*I would rather die on my feet
with honor than live
on bended knees in shame.*
—BENIGNO S. AQUINO, JR.
1973—TO THE MILITARY TRIBUNAL, FORT BONIFACIO

*If it were done when 'tis done,
then 'twere well
It were done quickly.*
—MACBETH, ACT I.

"*...Inasmuch as ye have done it
unto one of the least of my brethren,
ye have done it unto me.*"
MATTHEW, 25:40.

Published by: Hilltop Publishing Company
P.O. Box 654
Sonoma, California 95476

Cover Design by: Michael Hollyfield

ISBN 0-912133-04-X

First Printing December, 1983
Printed in the United States of America

AQUINO ASSASSINATION

The True Story and Analysis of the
Assassination of
Philippine Senator
Benigno S. Aquino, Jr.

by

Gerald N. Hill
and
Kathleen Thompson Hill
with the cooperation of Steve Psinakis

HILLTOP PUBLISHING COMPANY

CONTENTS

FOREWORD

I.   Young Man in a Hurry / 3

II.   Politics: Manila Style / 17

III.   Aquino in Exile / 13

IV.   Ninoy Comes Home / 25

V.   Open and Shut Case / 31

VI.   Not So Instant Replay / 39

VII.   Method out of Madness / 45

VIII.   Hard Evidence: The Camera Doesn't Lie / 53

IX.   Hard Evidence: Sound and Fury / 89

X.   Softer Evidence: The Eye-witnesses / 101

XI.   Ballistics and Bouncing Bullets / 107

XII.   The Smoking Gun / 115

XIII.   Galman: Villain or Victim / 123

XIV.   If at First... / 131

XV.   Commission and Omission / 139

XVI.   The Great Undercover Agent / 145

XVII.   Fourth Contingency Plan / 149

XVIII. Testimony Under Oath / 157

XIX.   A Matter of Succession / 169

XX.   Manilagate: The Conspiracy / 173

XXI.   Manilagate: The Coverup / 189

XXII.   The View from Malacanang / 197

        Ninoy Aquino in His Own Words / 209

        Commentary by Steve Psinakis / 217

        About the Authors / 224

Note

This book was made possible by the cooperation of Steve Psinakis and a group of researchers and correspondents of the U.S.-based Ninoy Aquino Movement for Freedom, Peace and Democracy.

Psinakis and the NAMFPD, without restraint or limitation, provided to the authors video and sound tapes, reports, photographs, sonograms, private interviews, transcripts of radio and television programs, documents, and press clippings from around the world.

While credit for gathering the massive amount of material is especially due Psinakis and the NAMFPD, the analysis, opinions, and conclusions expressed in this book are strictly those of the authors, who are not affiliated with or otherwise obligated to the NAMFPD.

Foreword

Senator Benigno S. Aquino, Jr. was the only statesman in modern times who voluntarily returned to his homeland while facing a death sentence. He returned to the Philippines after three years in exile and seven years in solitary confinement, to seek "the middle way between authoritarian corruption and communist temptation."

As the acknowledged leader of the moderate opposition to the authoritarian rule of President Marcos, Aquino risked his life to help restore democracy. The instant he stepped from the plane onto his own soil, he was shot in the back of the head.

The life and death of Benigno S. Aquino, Jr. were most unusual.

For 11 years he had not been permitted a single free step on his native Philippine soil, yet millions of people marched on foot with the cortege to his funeral.

"Ninoy" Aquino—an articulate populist politician turned Gandhi-like philosopher—was the living symbol of hope for democracy not only to Filipinos but to all those who suffer under the heel of totalitarian dictatorship throughout the world.

His was the voice of reconciliation, of peace-making and orderly transition back to democracy.

Senator Aquino's death was unusual because it was a savage blow against democracy itself.

His death was unusual because it took place in a 30-second period cut off from all news media and the eyes of the world, shrouded in mystery and rumor.

"Ninoy" Aquino either died at the hands of a cheap gun-for-hire who in turn was shot himself, or Aquino was the victim of a conspiracy at the highest levels of government to commit political murder.

Because Senator Aquino's life was remarkable the world deserves to know the truth about his death.

Young Man in a Hurry

As is true in many countries where large families are an institution, second cousins become friends and even sometimes marry without the Western stigma attached to the practice for medical or religious reasons.

Such was the case of Aurora and Senator Benigno Aquino, Sr. married in 1930. Benigno Aquino, Sr. was a widower who interrupted Aurora's quest for a degree in education at the University of the Philippines with a proposal of marriage.

Benigno Aquino, Sr. brought with him two sons and two daughters from his first marriage, and he and Aurora had seven children together in the following order: Maur, Ninoy (Benigno Jr.), Ditas, Lupita, Butz, Paul and Tessie (Teresa).

In a land where nicknames and diminuitives are not only fashionable but almost mandatory by custom, "Ninoy" was given to Benigno Jr. by his grandfather Servillano who took two syllables from the name BeNIgNO and added a Y at the end to connote affection. Servillano was a well-known "insurrecto" who fought against the Spanish and then the Americans at the turn of the century.

Benigno Aquino, Sr. was a Senator, Speaker of the Assembly, and a Cabinet Minister. He died in 1947, when Ninoy was 13, and from that time Ninoy worked with his half brother Billy, as he was said to be too proud to ask for an allowance.

As a *Manila Times* cub reporter barely out of secondary

school, Aquino went to Korea at age 17 as a war correspondent after his mother was advised by Dr. Jose Laurel that "It will make a man of him."[1]

Ninoy's widowed mother had returned to school and earned a Bachelor of Science Degree in Social Work from the Centro Escolar University in Manila, became active in social work, and eventually served as a national president of the Catholic Women's League from 1957 to 1960.

Ninoy married Corazon Cojuangco from his home town of Concepcion when they were both 21. Cory was from the large Cojuangco copra (coconut) growing family. Togther they enjoyed a sizeable wealth that let Ninoy pursue public service while raising a family. Unlike Ferdinand and Imelda Marcos', the Aquino wealth preceded his entry into politics.

The honeymoon was scarcely over when he took his first try at politics and was elected Mayor of Concepcion, Tarlac province when he was only 22. He was always the young man in a hurry, arriving at birth ten days earlier than expected.

At age 28 Aquino was elected Governor, the youngest in the history of Tarlac province, and in 1966, at age 34 he became the youngest Senator in the Philippines on the ticket of the Liberal Party. Only a year earlier Ferdinand Marcos had been elected President of the Philippines under the Nationalista Party banner. Elected separately as Vice President on the Nationalista ticket was Fernando Lopez, who brought both great influence and money to the party ticket.

Even as a young man, Aquino had developed a solid personal philosophy which interrelated elements of Christian teachings, justice and human dignity. Although the depth of his understanding of the human condition would further mature during years of confinement and exile, from the beginning his political activity was grounded in concerns much deeper than mere ambition.

---

1. "Interview with Ninoy's Mother, Aurora A. Aquino," *Mr. & Ms.*, September 23, 1983, Manila (Republic of the Philippines).

Nevertheless it was as a politician that he made his mark. The ready smile, the unruly cowlick of dark hair appearing like a Filipino Kennedy, the sheer energy of Aquino made him stand out as a leader. But most of all he was an orator whose strong voice and ready wit could galvanize a crowd while his intellect and reason stimulated the mind. At political rallies he was usually the last to speak. As one former Senator remembers, no one would leave until Ninoy finished speaking because he would always produce an exciting and stimulating stemwinder that would bring the crowd to its feet.

Having subdivided family land and given individual plots to field workers, Aquino was a man of proven principle who was both charismatic and a skilled political organizer who stood in the forefront of the Liberal Party by 1971. Senator Aquino was expected to be the victorious presidential candidate in the 1973 elections after President Marcos completed his second term.

Under the Constitution of the Republic of the Philippines in 1971, President Ferdinand Marcos could not run again.

CHAPTER 2

Politics Manila Style

During the 1971 Philippines congressional campaign, two fragmentation grenades were thrown onto the stage of a rally for Liberal Party Senatorial candidates running in opposition to Marcos' Nationalista. The place: Plaza Miranda, Manila. The date: August 21, 1971 – 12 years to the day before Benigno Aquino, Jr. would die.

The grenades exploded before the candidates began to speak, killing several bystanders and severely wounding three of the most prominent Marcos oppositionists: Senators Jovito Salonga, Sergio Osmena, Jr. (1969 Presidential candidate) and Ramon Mitra, all of whom still carry the scars and shrapnel.

On the following day President Marcos claimed the bombing was the work of Communists and pledged to track down the perpetrators of this crime. To this day the government contends it discovered nothing and no arrests were ever made.

Although several candidates were hospitalized, with Aquino and Liberal Party chief Senator Gerardo Roxas on the stump for the slate, the party actually gained seats in the fall elections. Soon thereafter Marcos began dropping hints that he had evidence that Senator Aquino was involved in the bombing of his own colleagues, apparently to counter the widespread rumor that Marcos was responsible.

A year later on the night of September 21, 1972, President Marcos declared martial law. In a well-coordinated sweep, ele-

7

ments of the armed forces shut down opposition newspapers, seized radio and television stations, arrested numerous opposition leaders and imprisoned thousands he considered a threat to his continuance in office. Within the first hour, Aquino was taken into custody while attending a meeting of party leadership at a downtown Manila hotel and taken to prison at Fort Bonifacio.

One of the last telephone calls to get out – before communications were temporarily shut down – was a call from Vice President Fernando Lopez to his industrialist brother, Eugenio Lopez, Sr. who was attending a bon voyage party in his honor in California on the eve of his return to the Philippines. "Do not come home," the Vice President told him. Within a short time Eugenio Lopez, Jr., director of the nation's largest television network and the *Manila Chronicle* followed Aquino into prison at Fort Bonifacio.

Other effects of martial law were the disbandment of Congress and the elimination of the office of Vice President.

A new constitution passed by a Marcos-dominated convention permitting Marcos to serve beyond his two terms was not long in coming.

Aquino was placed in solitary confinement at Fort Bonifacio, a military complex equipped with a prison used primarily by Marcos as a jail for major political prisoners. After almost a year in a legal limbo, Aquino was brought under heavy guard before a military court in August, 1973. There he heard the charges: murder, subversion (consorting with and abetting Communists), and illegal possession of firearms.

The Military Commission No. 2, comprised of a Brigadier General and five Colonels brushed aside the objections of Aquino's lawyers, including former Senators Salonga, Roxas and the venerable Lorenzo Tanada, that the military had no jurisdiction over a civil case.

Aquino stood before the court and announced he would not participate in the proceedings: "first, because this ritual is an unconscionable mockery; and second, because every part of my

8

being. . . is against any form of dictatorship. I agree we must have public order and national discipline, if the country is to move forward. But peace and order without freedom is nothing more than slavery. Discipline without justice is merely another name for oppression. I believe we can have lasting peace and prosperity only if we build a social order based on freedom and justice. My non-participation is therefore an act of protest against the structure of injustice that brought us here. It is also an act of faith in the ultimate victory of right over wrong, of good over evil. *In all humility, I say it is rare privilege to share with the Motherland her bondage, her anguish, her every pain and suffering.*"

He concluded: "Sirs, I know you to be honorable men. But the one unalterable fact is that you are the subordinates of the President. You may decide to preserve my life, but he can choose to send me to death. Some people suggested I beg for mercy. But this I cannot in conscience do. *I would rather die on my feet with honor than live on bended knees in shame.*"

Apparently fearful that Aquino would turn the trial into a forum for his considerable oratorical skills, Marcos postponed further hearings until 1975, when Aquino was again brought before the panel of army officers on April 4.

Senator Aquino again stated his protests against the right of a military tribunal to try him for accusations of civilian crimes, and announced that he would begin a hunger strike in protest.

The hunger strike device had been used in November of 1974 by the other two major political prisoners at Fort Bonifacio, Eugenio (Geny) Lopez, Jr. and Sergio Osmeña, III. After 11 days of their hunger strike, Defense Minister Juan Ponce Enrile assured Lopez and Osmena that a long list of political prisoners would be released and that they would be paroled as a first step toward freedom. Believing that they had gained at least a partial victory, the two agreed to halt their fasts.

Senator Aquino persisted in his hunger strike for 40 days, until he was almost comatose, when he was brought by the military to Veterans Hospital in Manila where he was first fed intravenously and eventually regained his strength. With his health restored, Aquino was returned to Fort Bonifacio where he remained for another two years before his military "trial" was resumed for a third time.

Aquino's sentence was announced in November of 1977: "Death by Musketry" (firing squad), and a storm of protest around the world was immediate. A petition of appeal to the military tribunal was filed and provided a ready excuse not to carry out the sentence immediately.

In early 1978, President Marcos called for the election of an "interim national assembly" on April 7. Benigno Aquino, Jr. filed from prison to run for the Assembly representing Manila, heading a slate of candidates calling themselves LABAN, which was both an acronym for Tagalog words meaning "People's Force," and a word itself for "fight."

During the campaign, Marcos seized upon Aquino's early training with the American CIA to warn the Filipino people against "certain opposition candidates who are backed by foreign governments." Defense Minister Juan Ponce Enrile, a favorite spokesman for Marcos at that time, alluded to the visit to Aquino by Patricia M. Derian, then American Under Secretary of State for Human Rights, sent by President Carter.

Quoting a transcript of a taped conversation between a Philippine intelligence officer and Aquino obtained by bugging Ninoy's cell, Minister Enrile cited Aquino's interest in the military strength of the Communists in the Philippines, his CIA training, and his one-time friendship with CIA Director Richard Helms, as implications of his subversive inclinations.

Since these were accusations made during a political campaign, Aquino demanded, through his wife and lawyers, a right to respond. Marcos agreed, with the stipulations that all questions would be asked by newsmen and that Aquino make no direct criticism of Marcos.

On the evening of March 10, 1978, prisoner Aquino faced the media from prison. The questioning immediately focused on the claim that he had been a CIA agent. The hand-chosen reporters weren't ready for the articulate Aquino.

Aquino responded that the contacts he had with the CIA in Africa and Indonesia had been fact-finding missions at the request of the president of the Philippines in the late 50's and early 60's. In turn he charged that the Marcos' public relations firm in Washington, D.C. was itself loaded with ex-CIA agents.

Thus, in one answer, Aquino succeeded in reviving memories of his patriotic service to his country, while branding the Marcoses as being in league with the CIA themselves.

As to communist connections, Aquino responded with righteous indignation that the principal testimony against him had been from a self-confessed murderer, who had been shot by the police in "mysterious circumstances" after testifying against him.

By the end of the program Aquino was in complete command. Whether intellectually perfect or not, his response and counter-attack were a brand of hard, effective political oratory that would not be forgotten.

But even more memorable was the effect of Aquino's appearance on the people of Manila. On that night, the city of millions slowed to a crawl, streets and bustling nightclubs were virtually deserted, as millions stayed indoors to watch him. In the slum districts, television sets mounted on crates or oil drums in the streets drew thousands. From the depths of prison Marcos' nemesis had reached out to the millions.

President Ferdinand Marcos would not forget it.

Nor would anyone forget the "noise barrage" on April 6, the eve of the election. A modest proposal that Aquino supporters make a little noise so he could hear he was not alone, turned into a demonstration. Tens of thousands clogged the streets of Manila, honking car horns, banging pans and chanting "Ninoy, Ninoy" long into the night. The foreign press called it a "moral victory" for the "people's force" whether the votes were counted or not.

Hours after the polls closed on election day, before the Commission on Elections could have counted the votes, Marcos announced on television that Imelda Marcos and the rest of their slate in Manila had won a clean sweep of all contested 21 seats in the city.

11

Even if the votes had been counted, the results would have been heavily pro-Marcos since the "People's Force" only ran 21 candidates for the 200 positions open. But Marcos' premature announcement foreclosed any possibility that a popular opposition candidate like Aquino could win even a single seat in the Assembly. As recently as a 1983 interview of Marcos on ABC after Aquino's death, Marcos claimed that Imelda had defeated Ninoy by "a million" votes.

Still under the death sentence and in solitary confinement at Fort Bonifacio in 1980, Senator Benigno Aquino, Jr. had become an embarrassment to the Marcos government. After the daring and dramatic escape from Fort Bonifacio by Geny Lopez and Sergio Osmena in the Fall of 1977, Aquino was the only non-Communist major political figure under detainment.

Fellow prisoners Lopez and Osmena had been held primarily as hostages. Lopez was the Marcos' bargaining point a) forcing the powerful Lopez family to remain silent and b) acquisition of much of their corporate holdings. Osmena's captivity bought the continued pacifity of his father, Senator Sergio Osmena, Jr., the son of a former President of the Philippines, who was in the United States for treatment of the aftermath of the wounds he received at the Plaza Miranda bombing.

The Lopez/Osmena escape, involved long preparations of removal of a barred window of Fort Bonifacio, dashing in the dark for an old airstrip, a daredevil snatching up of the two men by a private plane which smuggled them into Hong Kong, and their eventual transport to the United States by commercial airliner.

But Senator Aquino remained in solitary confinement.

CHAPTER 3

Aquino In Exile

After seven years and seven months in solitary confinement at Fort Bonifacio, Aquino was "released" on May 8, 1980, in what appeared to be a sudden stroke of humanitarianism. Military escorts put Aquino on a Philippine Airline flight from Manila to San Francisco.

A mild heart attack had revealed that Senator Aquino was in need of a delicate and urgent form of triple by-pass heart surgery. The operation he required was of such a nature that Aquino refused to allow the doctors at the military hospital to perform the surgery.

Imelda Marcos personally reviewed the medical reports on Aquino's condition and visited him in the hospital and was convinced by Aquino that she and her husband should allow him to travel to the United States rather than die at the hands of government surgeons. While Aquino was en route to the United States, it was announced in Manila daily newspapers that Marcos had given him a "temporary release" for "humanitarian reasons."

By releasing his arch political rival and exporting him to the United States for what was thought to be risky surgery and a "humanitarian" exile, Marcos believed that he had removed his biggest threat in future elections from physical as well as political effectiveness.

Aquino's triple by-pass surgery was performed successfully at Baylor University Medical Center in Texas, and he recovered with more vigor than even the medical experts had predicted.

Not only had Ninoy survived the surgery and recovered wholesomely, but he was offered and accepted prestigious fellowships at Harvard University and the Massachusetts Institute of Technology.

While one of the conditions of his "release" was that he not speak out while in the United States, Aquino decided three months later that his duty to his people was more important than "a pact with the devil." He lectured, studied and wrote about historic and current peaceful transitions from dictatorships to democracies. He travelled to many countries of the world to discuss and discover possible solutions for the return to democracy in the Philippines. He served as a peacemaker among exiled representatives of warring factions within the Philippines and spoke out in attempts to inform the world about what life was really like in his native land.

It was during this period of exile that Aquino reached a fuller political maturity. Like the best public men he had "grown." He had made the journey from charismatic politician to statesman of the world. Ninoy had studied Gandhi's works during his seven years imprisonment and after watching the movie "Gandhi," he told UPI reporter Max Vanzi that he had found the embodiment of all he had believed – peace, human concern and moral leadership.

Although martial law had been lifted technically, Marcos ruled by decree, with a rubber stamp parliament and a Supreme Court which never ruled against him on any issue. (After Aquino's death, the Court actually ruled against the government on the issue of giving permits for peaceful parades.)

Watching the growing size and influence of the military under Marcos on the one hand and the increased numbers of radical guerillas in the hinterlands, Aquino became increasingly concerned that democracy would not be restored. He could no longer stay on the sidelines.

On December 16, 1980, Senator Aquino met with Imelda Marcos in New York. During that meeting Mrs. Marcos showed Senator Aquino a film of a dinner she recently had hosted honoring ex-President Nixon and is reported to have pointed out several prominent people among the guests and stated that Nixon was back in the Reagan camp. In the videotape shown Senator Aquino by Mrs. Marcos, Nixon praises her grandly and refers to her as "The Angel from Asia."

Aquino related to Steve Psinakis that in his December meeting with Imelda Marcos, "She told me that you and I have sent assassination teams to Manila to knock off some of her people. She said if we do, they'll do the same to us and no one will come out ahead. She told me we should put a stop to that. . . . She sounded confident that the Reagan administration will go after us here, especially you."[1]

Thus, as related in Aquino's conversation with Psinakis, Mrs. Marcos was not only threatening a Senator named Aquino from her own country, but she was also claiming influence with two American Presidents to bring about harm to an American citizen. Three days later she reiterated the threats to Psinakis.

Sometime in May of 1983, Aquino made a firm decision to return home, which was the third of the conditions demanded by Marcos upon his "release" from solitary confinement earlier.

Aquino believed that Marcos was the key to a peaceful resolution to the unrest, lack of democracy, brutal killings, corruption, and the restoration of basic human rights and a sound economy to the Filipino people. From reports of the deterioration of the Philippine economy as well as Marcos' health, Aquino believed that time was of the essence, and that he must make an attempt to convince Marcos of the importance of a peaceful national reconciliation.

---

1. *Two Terrorists Meet*, by Steve Psinakis, Alchemy Press, San Francisco, 1980.

Apparently Aquino's decision prompted much hand-wringing within Malacañang Palace, the presidential residence. Having believed that they had removed this charismatic political threat from their lives, what would the Marcos' do if he had the nerve to fulfill his commitment in honor and return to his homeland?

Ninoy's fellowships at both Harvard and MIT expired in June of 1983, and rather than renew them for an additional year which would include the possible upcoming elections in the Philippines, Aquino decided this was the time to make his break and return to the Philippines.

Should his peacemaking efforts fail to convince Marcos that democratic reforms were essential for the future of the Philippines, Aquino was prepared to organize the Philippine opposition for the parliamentary elections scheduled for May, 1984.

In late 1982, both Aquino and Imelda Marcos attended a wake in New York for former Senator Gerardo Roxas who was eventually buried in the Philippines. During a breakfast meeting the day after the wake, Senator Aquino mentioned that his passport was expiring and Mrs. Marcos said she would take care of it. Aquino gave her his passport, but it was never returned to him or renewed.

Meanwhile, the death sentence imposed by the military tribunal in November, 1977, had been declared moot and academic after his departure for the United States. In July, 1983, the death sentence was again reaffirmed by President Marcos.

In a meeting at the Philippine Center in New York on May 21, 1983, Imelda Marcos reportedly made several statements and offers to Aquino.

He mentioned to Mrs. Marcos that he might go home, since his fellowships were completed and he wanted to return to his homeland rather than renew them for another year.

Rumors persist that Mrs. Marcos offered Senator Aquino the position of Prime Minister if he would join the Marcos government.

In another proposal to Aquino by Mrs. Marcos during the

May meeting, she offered to set Aquino up in business if he stayed in the U.S. This she confirmed in an interview with international press representatives in Manila, as reported in the September 30, 1983 issue of *Mr. & Ms.* of Manila.

"Question: Going back to your meeting with the senator . . . I'd just like to confirm if it's true that you offered him financial assistance so he can. . . . (inaudible)."

"FL (First Lady): Well, he said, in a way he said that President Reagan terminated his Harvard grant. He was suspecting that President Reagan terminated his Harvard grant, and so I said that if you really have difficulty in your stay here, I'm even ready to help you. It's true."

In reality, Senator Aquino was hoping to come home to attempt a peaceful reconciliation and improvement of life in a democracy in the Philippines. He saw the possibility of organizing a legitimate opposition political party and then campaigning for four months before the parliamentary elections in May of 1984.

Mrs. Marcos' final attempt at dissuading Aquino from returning to his motherland was to tell him not to come home because, she said, there were plots to kill him.

Even before that meeting, Marcos had urged Aquino to remain in the United States. As part of the apparent lifting of martial law in January, 1981, Presidential elections were set for June, 1981. Still ruling by decree, there was no chance that Marcos could lose. He publicly challenged Aquino to run against him, but privately sent former Senator Lorenzo M. Tanada to the United States in February, 1981, to tell Aquino that he would be re-arrested if he came back.

Despite Imelda's scarcely veiled threat in May, 1983, Aquino applied for travel papers in June, but the Philippine Consulate in New York refused with the excuse that military intelligence had uncovered an assassination plot.

In July, Deputy Foreign Minister Pacifico Castro warned all international air carriers not to allow Aquino to board their planes without proper documentation at the risk of losing their landing rights in the Philippines. Specifically Japan Air Lines was told it could lose its flight privileges to the Philippines if it carried Aquino. Ninoy joked that they were trying to force him to take Philippine Airlines and "I won't do it."

On August 2, Defense Minister Juan Ponce Enrile cabled Aquino to delay his return for "at least a month, because I have been directed to inform you that we are convinced beyond reasonable doubt that there are plots against your life upon your arrival in the Philippines." Aquino's public response was that he would meet them half way and delay two weeks to August 21. That should give them time to catch any plotters, he said, and at the same time it would give his friends and relatives in the Philippines the needed time to prepare a public welcome. On a Sunday his supporters would not be working and could meet him at Manila International Airport.

But Aquino's campaign timetable of four months to organize the opposition and four months to campaign was getting tight.

Aquino at military trial in 1973 with his lawyers.

A reunion with fellow political prisoners from Fort Bonifacio, Geny Lopez and Serge Osmena, while on way to Houston; Steve Psinakis at right.

Aquino addresses Los Angeles World Affairs Council, February 13, 1982.

Ninoy jogs with his doctor after by-pass surgery.

Jaime Cardinal Sin blesses body of Senator Aquino.

Corazon Aquino

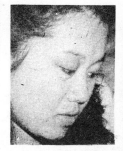

Aurora Corazon Aquino

Maria Elana Aquino

. Christina Aquino

Victoria Elisa Aquino

Benigno Aquino III

21

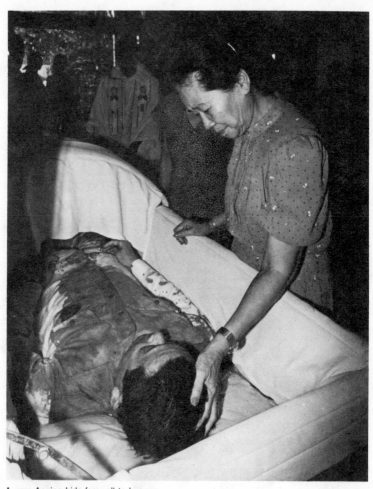

Aurora Aquino bids farewell to her son.

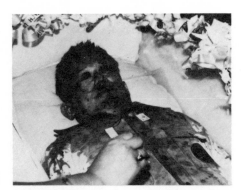

Senator Aquino in his coffin with his exit wound and abrasions showing.

A bereaved supporter on route of cortege to cemetery.

Millions pay final tribute to Senator Aquino.

CHAPTER 4

Ninoy Comes Home

Aquino flew from Boston to Los Angeles on Saturday, August 13. Apparently the Philippine government had been monitoring his movements because by the next day they were trying to locate him.

Senator Aquino was armed with a counterfeit passport he had obtained in "a Muslim country" which bore the name "Marcial Bonifacio." According to his brother-in-law, Ken Kashiwahara, Ninoy took great delight in the name since it stood for martial law and his old prison, Fort Bonifacio.

Hoping to keep the Philippine government in the dark he moved from Singapore to Malaysia, back to Singapore and finally to Taipei, capital of Taiwan, on Friday, August 19, where he was met by brother-in-law Kashiwahara, an American ABC newsman on vacation. Ken's wife Lupita and another of Ninoy's sisters, Tessie, already preceded him to Manila to help organize a homecoming reception.

Taipei had been chosen as the final embarkation point because it did not have diplomatic relations with the Philippines which reduced the chance of discovery by Philippine officials. From his hotel Senator Aquino telephoned friends in the Philippines. For purposes of security this was a dicey business since overseas calls to prominent opposition people are known to be monitored and a system of "safe" phones is often used, but overseas calls are sometimes spot-checked by government security forces. In one of these calls Aquino was told he might be shot at the airport.

Fearful that the call could alert the Nationalist China government, which might not allow him to board the plane, an intermediary checked with the government and was told, "We have never heard of Aquino and we do not know he is in Taiwan."

Aquino believed that being accompanied by journalists was beneficial from two standpoints: it would insure that his story would gain maximum publicity even if he were kept on the plane or jailed on his return, and the media's presence would lessen the possibility of an attempt on his life. By Saturday about ten journalists had congregated in Taipei to accompany Senator Aquino on the final leg of his journey home. And later in the afternoon of August 20, the group was joined by two television crews from Japan.

In another call from Manila on Saturday, Aquino was told that opposition leaders would not be allowed to meet him at the plane. "That's a bad sign," he told his brother-in-law, interpreting it as meaning the plane might be turned around upon landing without letting him out, or that he might be taken away to prison incommunicado. He told Kashiwahara when they were alone that he felt assassination was only a remote possibility, but nonetheless showed him a bullet proof vest.

"But if they hit me in the head, I'm a goner."

It was after midnight before Aquino drifted off to sleep, still fingering his rosary. Four hours later he was up for a telephone call to his wife and children in Boston. She read a Bible passage to him and he spoke briefly with each child. As he talked to them he began to cry. After hanging up, Senator Aquino wrote a letter to each of his children.

By the time Aquino reached the Chiang Kai Check International Airport at 10:10 a.m., his spirits had revived. His car circled the airport so he could arrive at the last minute while Kashiwahara and a friend checked through the luggage of "Marcial Bonifacio."

Aquino got through immigration without difficulty, and then

two Chinese officials pulled him aside. His brother-in-law behind him at the immigration desk thought the entire trip was over.

"That was the Taiwan garrison commander," Ninoy told Ken with a big smile, "he just wanted to make sure I got through OK. But he said something very curious. He said he was called by Philippine Airlines this morning and was told to take good care of me."

China Airlines Flight 811 for Manila, a Boeing 767 carrying over a hundred passengers, cleared Taipei at 11:15 a.m.

Meanwhile in Manila busloads of opposition supporters had begun arriving at Manila International Airport. Yellow ribbons were draped over the buses and jeeps and around trees, and the friends of Aquino could be identified by yellow ribbons, a symbol from the song about the return of the freed prisoner, "Tie A Yellow Ribbon Round the Old Oak Tree."

Some of the grand old names of the opposition were on hand, as well as the Senator's 73 year-old mother, Aurora Aquino, and his sisters, brothers and more than 20,000. Family and close friends were crowded into a V.I.P. Lounge, while thousands filled the parking lot.

At 11:30 a.m. television cameramen and other reporters on hand were ordered to congregate at the entrance to the tunnel of the jetway at Gate 8, and further told not to leave that location.

Symbolically wearing the same white safari suit he had worn the day of his trip to Houston three years before, Aquino spent much of the trip talking to the press. At one point two pretty young Filipino women made their way down the aisle and kissed Aquino on the cheek. They were laughing as they wiped away the lipstick smudge. Ninoy laughed along also, and instantly became the politician again, shaking their hands and wishing them well.

As the plane reached the shore of Luzon Island, Aquino, sitting in seat 14C on the aisle, prayed to himself, his fingers sliding along the beads of his rosary.

The China Airliner began the descent over rice fields and

27

villages. Aquino went to the rest room and put on the bullet proof vest and covered it with his white shirt and safari jacket.

He handed his gold watch to his brother-in-law.

"I just want you to have it," he said.

"Don't forget to go to my house as soon as we land and have someone take my belongings to me in prison." He told Kashiwahara that in the bag were four days of clothes for the first few days in prison.

When the plane touched down Kashiwahara said: "Ninoy, we're home," and Aquino looked up and smiled.

As the plane swung around toward the jetway to Gate 8 a crowd could be seen beyond the main terminal. Alongside the plane a blue AVSECOM van pulled up and members of teams Alfa, Bravo and Charlie surrounded the plane, all facing out away from the plane with rifles at the ready.

As the motors were shut off, three men entered the passenger compartment – one in the uniform of the Philippine Constabulary and two with AVSECOM patches on their khaki uniforms. The Constabulary man passed Aquino, but an AVSECOM guard recognized him and leaned forward and shook his hand, mumbling something in Tagalog – the word "boss" was distinguishable. The time was 1:14 p.m.

The ABC and TBS television crews pushed forward to catch the scene. As Aquino rose from his seat, one of the AVSECOM men took his small bag and the other took a firm grip on his arm and started to lead him down the aisle.

Kashiwahara got up and started to follow, stating: "I'm coming with him. I'm his brother-in-law."

An AVSECOM man wearing sunglasses told him abruptly: "You just take seat," and turned to follow Aquino.

Aquino had been smiling, but suddenly his face took on a stoney, melancholic expression. His mouth became a grim line.

The television crews and reporters Wakamiya and Matsumoto pressed after them with cameras rolling. Kashiwahara and other reporters followed. Standing facing the interior of the plane was a plainclothes security man. Inside the entrance of

28

the tunnel to the main terminal were two more uniformed men, one from the Constabulary and one from AVSECOM, as well as four to six more plainclothesmen dressed in white "polo barongs."

Suddenly a side door on the left of the tunnel was opened to a stairway to the ground. The AVSECOM man in the sunglasses, who had told Kashiwahara to "take seat" was at Aquino's elbow, and the soldier holding his wrist was at his right. The two men swung Ninoy out onto the platform and were followed by two of the uniformed men and a plainclothesman in a white shirt. A second security man, also in a white "polo barong" shirt, stepped out onto the platform with his back to the reporters.

As Senator Aquino disappeared from view, the remaining uniformed soldier and several plainclothesmen quickly blocked the doorway to the stairs with their bodies.

As the TBS television crewmen tried to lift their camera over their heads, the hands of a plainclothesman came forward to cover the lens, while audio booms from both television crews swung high in the air aimed toward the open doorway.

The media men pushed, shoved, and jockeyed for position.

Bang. A single gunshot, loud and ominous.

A woman screamed.

There was pandemonium among the people around the stairway door. Reporter Wakamiya heard the shot and saw Aquino fall forward like a log. Trapped in the aisle, reporter Ueda looked out the window after the sound of the shot and saw Aquino on the ground, his neck spouting blood.

It was 50 seconds since Benigno Aquino, Jr. had risen from seat 14 C. He had come home for the last time.

CHAPTER 5

Open and Shut Case

The official government version of the death of Senator Aquino was extremely simple. Witnesses said that as he was being taken by security men from the side stairs by the jetway to a waiting AVSECOM van, a man in his twenties dressed in blue denims and white (actually light blue) shirt rushed from around the front of the plane. He shot Aquino once in the back of the head from behind. The murder weapon was a .357 Smith & Wesson revolver. Security men immediately opened fire on the assailant with automatic rifles and killed him. The killer was yet to be identified.

That was the story told at the press conference at Manila International Airport (MIA) held by Major General Prospero Olivas, Philippine Constabulary Metrocom Chief, at 5:15 p.m., four hours after the murder. Although the government's story would be fleshed out over the next few weeks, there was no great variation from that basic narrative. Olivas had been appointed to investigate the assassination by General Fabian Ver, Chief of Staff of the Armed Forces.

Also at the press conference was Brigadier General Luther Custodio, AVSECOM chief, who sat dandling the .357 magnum in his hand while Olivas spoke.

The newspapers reported that Aquino had been taken immediately in the AVSECOM van to the army hospital at Fort Bonifacio, but he was dead on arrival. News photos taken less than a minute after the shooting showed Senator Aquino lying on his face, as if headed for the van, with his feet about seven feet from the foot of the side stairs to the jetway. Approximately two feet from his bloodied head – angling to the left and in front of Aquino's body – lay the dead "assailant" on his back.

Olivas announced that several "eyewitnesses" were being interrogated. AVSECOM's General Custodio said that he had been instructed to arrest Aquino and bring him to the Military Security Command for custody under Major General Josephus Ramas, Army chief.

During the afternoon, reporters had been shown the dead body of the "assassin" as it lay on the tarmac for several hours. Beside the body they spotted spent armalite (M16) shells, a .45 shell and five unused bullets fitting a .357 magnum.

Olivas spent most of the rest of the interview complaining that Aquino had ignored repeated warnings not to return to the Philippines because of threats on his life.

At 7:00 p.m. President Marcos issued a statement in which he lamented that Aquino had not heeded the warnings not to return "until we could clear the way for his arrival." Marcos excused the failure to protect Aquino and at the same time alluded to the type of killer involved: "The protection of a public official's life against a determined killer who is ready to die in the attempt at assassination will always be one of the most difficult, if not impossible, tasks of security men in the world."

Marcos also pledged that the government would apply "all its resources and powers" to bring to justice those responsible "in the quickest possible time."

That was it, open and shut case. They had the killer, dead. They had the weapon. They had eyewitnesses. They had the excuse: You cannot stop an assassin willing to give his life. Just a few loose ends: 1) identity of assailant, 2) whether he had confederates, and 3) what was his motive. The government would shortly have it all wrapped up.

An autopsy on the body of Benigno Aquino was performed

at 10:00 p.m. that night in the Loyola Memorial Chapel Morgue by Dr. Bienvenido O. Munoz, medical-legal officer of the National Bureau of Investigation. Representatives of the Aquino family were present as witnesses.

Death was caused by a single bullet which entered Aquino's head behind the left ear with an entrance of 0.7 to 0.8 centimeters (less than one-third inch). The bullet was "directed forward, downward, and medially" fracturing several bones on the way and passing through a lobe of the brain. It exited in the chin (mandible) leaving a hole 1.5 by 0.8 centimeters (six-tenths of an inch by one-third of an inch).

There was an area of tatooing (powder burns) around the bullet entrance of three to six centimeters (1.2 inches by 2.3 inches). Three metal fragments were found, one imbedded in bone and two near the exit point.

Abrasions and contusions were found on Aquino's right eyelid, left temple, upper lip, and left shoulder, with pinpoint bruises on his forehead and cheek.

Senator Aquino's height was listed at 169 centimeters (five feet six inches), although his actual height was five feet nine inches.

Meanwhile at the Philippine Constabulary Crime Laboratory an autopsy of the unknown assailant's body began at 11:20 p.m. under the direction of another medical-legal officer of the National Bureau of Investigation, Dr. Nieto M. Salvador. The computer printout of the heading page of the autopsy is shown in figure 4.

Dr. Salvador listed eight wounds in the assailant. The first was behind and above the left ear, penetrating the cranial cavity. Wounds 2, 3 and 4 were all frontal, basically in the chest. Number 5 was at the "back of chest." Wound 6 was described as specifically in the back.

According to the medical examiner wound 7 was apparently a single wound with nine perforations from stomach to right thigh on the basis that the shot was from a "prone shooter."

Number 8 was in the elbow region (which elbow was not stated). Finally, he had been grazed by two other shots without reference to location.

Within the body – without reference to location – were found a total of seven bullets. Four were "deformed jacketed" bullets, two were "slightly deformed jacketed" bullets and one was a "deformed copper jacket." These had been turned over to the investigative section of the National Bureau of Investigation.

The autopsy also revealed that the assailant's stomach was filled up to one-third with partially digested rice. His height was listed on the printout as 175 centimeters (five feet ten inches).

Cause of death was stated as "shock secondary to multiple gunshot wounds."

If the authorities thought they would be able to file the autopsy reports, identify the killer, and close the file they were to be sorely disappointed. In the next few days there would be an unprecedented display of public outrage in the Philippines as the crescendo of the voices of mourners for the fallen Aquino rose, and the first of some very pointed questions were asked at home and around the world regarding the circumstances of his death.

The first persistent question was: How did the assailant penetrate the supposedly tight security to be in the area at all? And how was he able to sneak up behind Aquino to within 18 inches – as the powder burns would show – without being stopped?

Who was the assassin? What were his motives? Why did he not try to run away? Who was behind him? Why was he shot and killed rather than taken alive? And more ominously, could he have been used by the military or the government?

Why was Aquino suddenly taken down the side stairway of the jetway? How did the killer know he would be there? Why were the media representatives kept from seeing Aquino's movement to the AVSECOM van? Why were bullets pumped into the assassin after he was obviously dead? Did the killer shoot Aquino in the head because he knew he was wearing a bullet proof vest?

34

While tens of thousands passed by to view Benigno Aquino in his open casket on display at the home of his family, who had demanded that the bullet hole in his chin and the facial abrasions remain untouched by the mortician's ministrations, the government set about responding to these disturbing questions.

On the night of Monday, August 22, President Marcos told reporters that he hoped the opposition would not "exploit" the death of Aquino, and said that he did not intend to reimpose martial law as some rumors claimed he would. In regard to the motive for the killing, he said that it was possible that it was either to avenge the deaths of men who testified against the Senator in his trial or a plain communist "rubout," but he added, "the government will not make any conclusions until the problem is over."

General Olivas described the assassin as about five feet seven inches tall, and released a photo of the dead man's face, asking the public help in identifying him. He also announced that airport supervisors were looking for service personnel who might know something. Finally, he said that 14 members of AVSECOM assigned to the airport had been subjected to paraffin tests (to see if they had fired guns).

Marcos deplored reports by "foreign correspondents" that Aquino was shot by two of his guards.

On Tuesday General Olivas announced that the name "Rolly" had been embroidered on the dead assailant's briefs.

President Marcos was photographed confering with cabinet ministers on the investigation of the assassination, and was reported to have theorized that the killing was meant to embarrass his government.

Metrocom revealed that the killer had six extra bullets in his pocket and that the murder weapon contained five live bullets, three "lead semi-wad cutters" and two "semi-jacketed hollow" points. One Colonel Luis G. San Andres pointed out that "both types cut a wider swath" than ordinary bullets.

According to Metrocom, shell casings gathered off the tarmac at the scene of death included 24 armalite (M16) shells, and one from a .45 caliber pistol. Metrocom also stated that the National Bureau of Investigation was interpreting the entry and exit points on Aquino.

Wednesday's newspapers carried stories of interviews with James Gregor, professor of political science at the University of California in Berkeley and Dr. Guy Pauker, consultant of the Rand Corporation for the Philippines and Southeast Asia and a friend of Aquino. The two men had appeared on the MacNeil-Lehrer Report on PBS in the United States. Gregor and Pauker both said that the radical left benefited most from Aquino's death, and Gregor added that Marcos was "not a fool" and that to Marcos, Aquino was "less of a threat alive than assassinated."

That same day Marcos announced the appointment of a commission to look into the assassination, to be headed by Chief Justice Enrique Fernando, 68, and including four retired justices ranging in age from 68 to 80. Marcos announced the "grounding" of AVSECOM and assigned its duties to General Ver. He also authorized a half-million peso reward for information leading to the arrest of anyone linked to the slaying.

Corazon Aquino arrived in Manila and in a tearful press conference asked why only three men, who the government said were unarmed, had been assigned to guard her late husband.

Thursday afternoon, using many of the AVSECOM guards involved in the actual incident, Metrocom staged a televised re-enactment of the assassination on the tarmac at MIA.

That same day Brigadier General Luther Custodio, commanding general of AVSECOM had been ordered "confined to quarters," together with the escorts and 14 other AVSECOM personnel. The three men who entered the China airliner were identified as Metrocom Constable First Class Lazaga and Airmen deMesa and Lat.

Olivas stated that the National Bureau of Investigation had compared the three fragments found in Aquino's head, a deformed copper jacketed shell found at the scene and test bullets and found that the fragments came from the "death weapon." The government had previously announced that the revolver, originally shipped from Springfield, Massachusetts, by the manufacturer in 1970 had been hijacked in Thailand the same year and further tracing seemed impossible.

The general also reported that the inquiry continued to hit "blind leads."

However, several thousand miles away, in Tokyo, Japan, there loomed a more monumental problem for the official version and its re-enactors than "blind leads."

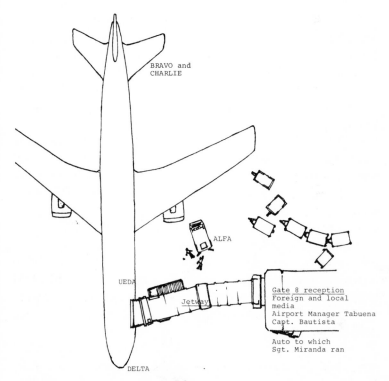

Layout of China Airliner and surrounding scene.

CHAPTER 6

Not So Instant Replay

Four days after the killing, on Thursday afternoon, August 25, a "re-enactment" of the assassination was videotaped at the scene under the direction of Metrocom Chief Olivas. The re-enactment film was shown on Manila television on Saturday night, August 27th. The participants in the film, according to the government, included many of the AVSECOM men who had been involved in the actual event.

General Olivas told the press on Saturday that the portrayal was intended to determine and demonstrate, if possible, how the assailant got through the security arrangements. He said that the film was accurate except that a different airliner had to be employed. The re-enactment showed clearly that the stairway was the 19-step metal ramp down which Aquino had been brought by his escorts.

As the scene opened, the AVSECOM van was in place and only three people were visible. One was apparently an airport employee in white overalls standing about 25 feet to the left of the van. Another man stood to the right under the plane at least 120 feet away. A third figure was momentarily visible behind the van, apparently representing an AVSECOM man waiting to open the van door.

Suddenly Senator Aquino appeared, wearing his distinctive white safari suit with a uniformed man gripping each of his arms and a third uniformed man behind him and slightly to the right.

It was a tight fit for three across on the stairway, so Aquino was held slightly in front of the two men grasping his arms. Aquino and the three men immediately started down the steps, moving very quickly. As they began the descent, two men in white polo barong shirts stepped out from the jetway onto the stairway platform and watched.

As Aquino reached the ground a figure in jeans and a light colored shirt could be seen emerging from somewhere back of the stairway. This man trotted around the stairway on the side toward the tail of the plane – pulling a pistol from his belt as he ran – and caught up with Aquino after the group had taken eight steps toward the van. Then he fired.

At the moment of the shooting, the man playing Aquino pitched forward onto the ground. The guard at Aquino's left dived away from him and lay face down on the tarmac. His escort on the right ran and hid against the right side of the van and the third guard raced out of camera view to the right.

The two men at the top of the stairs started running down when the shot was fired.

If isolated from the rest of the action, the movement of the alleged assassin was peculiar. After dealing the death shot, he began what can best be described as a pirouette, spinning away to Aquino's left. The man's arms were raised straight up in the air, and with one final turn he fell on his back to the left and in front of Aquino's body.

The alleged assailant then lay motionless on the ground while several blue-uniformed men jumped out of the rear door of the van. Two or three of them began firing at the man in jeans lying on the ground. At the same time, the guard of Aquino hugging the tarmac at the left leaped up and ran behind the van.

While the shooting of the man on the ground was going on, several other blue-uniformed men took stances similar to those shown in the still photo which had appeared in the Manila newspapers, aiming pistols and M16s in various directions.

In the government's re-enactment there was only one burst of concentrated gunfire at the alleged assassin. Then two more uniformed men leaped from the van door, picked up the man playing Aquino and tossed him into the back of the truck. The other uniformed men ran back and climbed aboard, the doors were swung shut, and the alleged killer's body was alone on the tarmac.

Re-enactments, even when using actual participants, are always difficult, particularly when several people are involved. In this case, the directors of the tableau had the advantage of knowing the original assignments of the various participants and therefore the approximate locations at the beginning of the camera's action. Those who had been involved had a fair idea what each had done – although in the excitement the memory may be less than perfect.

At the time it was aired the re-enactment videotape was the latest government statement as to what occurred at 1:15 p.m. Sunday when Aquino was brought down the stairs. The home audience would see it once, covering a period of 45 seconds. Fortunately, however, the government re-enactment was copied by ABC, broadcast in the United States, and made available for careful study like an instant replay of a scoring run in a baseball game.

Its directors had certain known or claimed "facts" which had to be fitted into the scenario. First, and most compelling, was the location of the bodies of Aquino and his alleged killer as photographed within a few seconds of their deaths. Second, at the time of the shooting, two of Aquino's escorts had him by the arms or elbows. Third, Aquino had been shot in the back of the neck by a single shot from a pistol. Fourth, the alleged killer had been shot numerous times and had ended up on his back.

At the time the re-enactment was made, the newspapers had carried reports that only three uniformed men had taken Aquino from his seat in the plane and still photos had shown the three taking him down the aisle. People within the plane had reported that a couple of white-shirted security men had obscured their vision at the doorway. Newspapers around the world had carried the dramatic picture of blue-uniformed AVSECOM men pointing pistols and rifles in all directions from professional shooting stances less than a minute after Aquino's death. This same picture and others taken about the same time had revealed that the khaki-uniformed escorts were nowhere in sight.

Finally, the scriptwriters had to show how the assassin was able to fire the fatal shot from less than two feet behind Aquino without being detected. They also had to depict how he failed to make any effort to get away or shoot it out with soldiers and security men.

The script called for all those elements and the final production got them in.

The most striking impression upon viewing the re-enactment was the almost complete absence of people on the landscape. Security was supposed to be "tight," and there had been soldiers running into position as the plane taxied to a stop. Yet only one soldier was in sight and he was in no position to do anything.

Next, the action of the supposed killer after firing the shot at Aquino made no sense except to get him on his back in the place where in reality he wound up. The apparent cowardice of the three guards of Aquino was startling, but, of course, not impossible.

The arrival on the scene of the alleged killer as acted out in the re-enactment raised as many questions as it answered. Since he came from beneath the stairs, why had he not been seen by the AVSECOM men who deployed as the plane's engines shut down? Why didn't the security men at the top of the steps or in the van see him and cry out a warning?

General Olivas and Colonel Hermogenes Peralta, Jr., criminal intelligence chief for the Constabulary, did not have the advantage of having viewed the three documentaries on the Aquino assassination which had played on Tokyo television's three networks after the re-enactment was produced. Tokyo Broadcasting System used its own videotape while Japan Broadcasting Network (Nippon Hoso Kyokai or NHK) and Asahi both employed the ABC camerawork.

As will be detailed, the Japanese videotapes showed that in contradiction to the re-enactment: 1) there were numerous uniformed men and apparent security men in white polo barongs (cool, white shirts open at the neck) at various locations outside the plane, 2) a fourth soldier and an agent in a polo barong had gone out the stairway door, and 3) there were two separate volleys of gunfire after the initial shot. In addition, the Japanese sound tracks would provide accurate timing of known events in relation to the gun shots.

The re-enactment videotape was timed by stopwatch. From his step onto the platform in the re-enactment until Aquino's foot touched the ground was 9.5 seconds. From the bottom of the stairs until he was shot eight footsteps away was timed at 4.5 seconds. Between the first fatal shot and the first shot by AVSECOM men leaping from the van at the prostrate figure of the alleged killer was another 4.5 seconds. While the assassin was spinning to the ground and lying there for approximately 3.0 seconds, several men in blue uniforms had jumped from the rear door of the van. The three escorts had also run away. The next 16.5 seconds included the shooting of the man on the ground, several men fanning out in a firing posture, and the further exit from the van of two more uniformed men who picked up Aquino's body and lifted it into the back of the van. By 36 seconds from the beginning of the re-play the van was pulling away.

On Monday, August 29, the *Philippines Daily Express* quoted General Olivas, who no doubt had heard of or about the Japanese videotapes, as saying that the re-enactment suffered from "some inaccuracies, such as the wrong type of plane and *the absence of several people* at the scene of the murder." (Emphasis added). He also asked journalists who had travelled with Aquino to help in a "second" re-enactment which he hoped that with their help would be more accurate. It was never made.

CHAPTER 7

Method Out Of Madness

The murder of Senator Aquino embodied many of the classic elements of a well-devised detective story. First of all, the reader/viewer was kept in the dark during the period of 30 to 40 seconds in which the actual deed occured. Where the novelist obliterates the action to maintain suspense, the question in the Aquino case was whether it was done by accident or design.

There were the suspects, the list of which may include the second body lying on the tarmac or any of a dozen other men in the vicinity. And in line behind the first rung of suspects are an almost infinite variety of other potential perpetrators: Communists, the military, government officials, those with a personal score to settle.

Next there was the murder weapon, or was it? There are enough spent shells lying about to fit a dozen weapons.

Witnesses: Six for the government who were "eyewitnesses," and then a host of people who had only a partial or fragmentary story to tell; excited, partisan, emotional, and often contradictory. There were rumors and second-hand reports of witnesses who were anonymous, unknown or at unrevealed locations. Like a cleverly-developed detective novel, all of the witnesses could not be telling the truth for their stories did not match. Was this confusion or duplicity? Were their errors merely human or venal?

And of course, there was the mystery of motive. In the

assassination of a political figure, motivation can run the gamut from insanity through revenge to calculated political purpose. A man like Senator Aquino could be envisioned as an enemy by both the right and the left, the communist and the plutocrat, the insider on the way up or the outsider resenting his intrusion and popularity. To determine a motive one must know the history, personal and political, of both victim and killer. To know the murderer one must understand the murderee.

But best of all, there was evidence. Properly examined, evidence can light the way to the truth. Unlike the mystery novel in which the solution is in the whimsical hands of the author, in real life truth is the singular and only possible conclusion. However, when a famous man dies under mysterious circumstances the truth is often shrouded in rumor, love, hate, lies, hysteria, irrelevancies and wild accusation. As Kipling warned his son: "If you can keep your head, when all about you are losing theirs . . ."

Therefore, it was vital to develop and employ a logical method in examining the great heap of evidence – and strange lack of data in some areas – which had already accumulated within a few days after Senator Aquino's death. The evidence would be primarily evaluated according to the standard rules of evidence employed by the courts, but also by other investigative techniques. These embody the historical knowledge of human conduct and physical possibility as well as rules of logic.

Roughly, evidence breaks down into the following categories:

1. Hard: uncontrovertible, physically provable evidence, which could not be contrived.

2. Make weight: Evidence which by itself may not prove anything, but when considered with hard evidence gives weight to certain conclusions or reinforces either hard or circumstantial evidence.

3. Circumstantial: This is evidence of circumstances that in the normal course of human conduct or natural laws would lead to particular conclusions. (If a man yawns he is in all

likelihood tired or bored, but it could be otherwise.) Circumstantial evidence must be particularly strong and convincing to lead to a conclusion. However, when found in conjunction with some hard evidence and substantive "make weight" evidence it can be particularly valuable.

4. Deductive evidence: This is not truly evidence, but has value in that by applying logic and/or reasonable assumptions to known facts, a solution may be found – or a fact deduced – for which there is no other answer. Thus, the answer can be used as evidence – although with great caution.

5. Absence of evidence: If there is no evidence of an occurrence which in the course of normal expectations of human conduct or physical laws should occur then this can lead to certain natural assumptions. While often given short shrift in court, spotting these gaps can be a valuable tool to the investigator.

6. Evidence that is not evidence: Rumor, mere speculation, unsupported opinion, obviously self-serving braggadocio or lies, or matters of complete irrelevance. All these may be examined but are of no real use. Yet they clutter the field and must be kept in mind, if only because on occasion the rumor, the opinion, the accusation turns out to be the shadow of reality.

In a criminal matter it is axiomatic that a witness – in or out of court – who knowingly lies or conceals a fact does so for a reason. Mere obscurity does not guarantee that there is a concealer. However, whenever it is clear that information is intentionally hidden or distorted, one should look for the reason. In a matter of murder it can only be to protect the guilty, deflect suspicion toward the innocent, or obscure one's perception.

Finally, it should be realized that just because there is a mystery or some matter unexplained this does not automatically mean there exists a plot or conspiracy. The investigator frustrated by "blind leads" and apparently conflicting data should only posit a conspiracy on hard evidence and a total lack of any other explanation.

One of the worst errors an investigator can make is to begin with a conclusion and work backwards to prove it is true, discarding or discounting evidence which does not conform to that prejudgment and seizing on the weakest link which supports it. To avoid this trap, the investigator should begin with the building blocks of hard evidence instead of hypotheses.

Thus, the authors began with hardest, most definitive evidence of all: The sights and sounds of the murder.

0:0 seconds—Aquino appears on platform.

6:0 seconds—Aquino halfway down stairs.

9:5 seconds – Aquino's foot touches ground.

Philippine Government
Reenactment

2:0 seconds – Galman appears from behind stairs.

Philippine Government
Reenactment

13:0 seconds – Galman pulls gun from belt.

14:0 seconds – moment of shooting; Galman behind guard on right.

14:5 seconds – Galman turning backwards and to left; Aquino still standing; Moreno running away; Lat stumbling.

16:0 seconds – Aquino face down; Galman has spun and fallen on back in shadow of van; deMesa lying down; Lat at right.

18:0 seconds—soldiers firing at Galman on ground at right and point in all directions; deMesa still on ground.

30:0 seconds—soldier lift Aquino into van; one is pointing gun at empty stairway.

CHAPTER 8

Hard Evidence: The Camera Doesn't Lie

On board China Airlines Flight 811 to Manila August 21, 1983, were two television crews based in Japan: Tokyo Broadcasting System (TBS) and American Broadcasting Company (ABC). Reporters with cameras included Katsuo Ueda of Kyodo News Service, Arthur Kan of *Asiaweek* of Hong Kong, Toshi Matsumoto and Kiyoshi Wakamiya.

Ninoy Aquino was of the firm opinion that having a large contingent of media people along was a protection. He felt that an attempt on his life or rough treatment in full view of the world's press representatives was virtually unthinkable. His theory was predicated on the belief that those waiting in Manila to take him to prison or otherwise deal with him would know that he would have media people on board.

During the trip the television crews had been taping interviews as well as casual conversations. The cameras went on again even before the airliner came to a rest at the jetway tunnel to Gate 8. Men in dark uniforms armed with rifles could be seen running alongside the plane apparently heading for assigned positions (TV-3 and TV-4). A dark blue van with windowed double doors and emblazoned with a shield and the acronym AVSECOM was parked close by (PIC-1). AVSECOM stands for Aviation Security Command which is a specialty unit originally organized to protect against skyjacking and to make airports secure against terrorists. It operates directly under the Armed Forces Chief of Staff General Fabian Ver.

Plainclothes security men wearing white polo barongs were in evidence. They could be seen with uniformed men under the jetway to the main terminal and a TBS camera picked up one standing under a metal flight of stairs from the side of the jetway (TV-5 and TV-6). When panning their cameras around the tarmac from the airliner windows, the cameramen had no idea how important that stairway would shortly become.

While some of the passengers began gathering up their belongings to disembark, the public address system asked them to remain on board. Then the cameras picked up three men dressed in khaki uniforms coming down the aisle. In the lead was a man later identified as Lazaga in the uniform of the Philippine Constabulary—the home army and Federal police force. Attached to his belt on the right was a buttoned down leather holster, clearly visible in the ABC videotape. The top of it can be seen in TV-6 and all of it in TV-8. This man passed by Aquino, but behind him an AVSECOM sergeant, a husky fellow in sunglasses (later identified as deMesa) spotted the Senator.

Sergeant deMesa seemed surprised to find the cameras on him and put his hand over his face and ducked his head (TV-9). Nevertheless, while UPI correspondent Max Vanzi looked on from the seat behind Aquino, deMesa reached around Aquino as if in a friendly gesture and expertly felt him for weapons and bullet proof vest (PIC-2). The third man in khaki, another AVSECOM man (later identified as Lat), whispered something in Tagalog to Aquino (TV-10).

Lat and deMesa began helping Aquino to his feet. When the ABC tape was used by NHK, that network put a timer on the picture beginning with Aquino's first move to get up. As he rose, deMesa took a firm grip on the strap to Aquino's overnight bag and Lat took his wrist.

Based on the usual deference of police and military to important people even when detainees, their conduct was surprising. When Aquino was arrested in 1972, he was "invited" to come with the police who were full of apologies; such political detainees as Geny Lopez and Serge Osmena tell of the same experience.

Suddenly Aquino's expression was of apprehension (TV–11).

Ken Kashiwahara, Aquino's brother-in-law, demanded of Lazaga that he be allowed to accompany Aquino. "I'm his brother-in-law." As Lazaga hesitated (TV–12), deMesa said sharply, "You just take seat." Wakamiya pushed in behind the television crews and Kashiwahara followed him.

Sergeant Lat, Aquino's left wrist held firmly, pulled Aquino along the aisle with deMesa gripping an arm in his meaty fist and Lazaga brought up the rear. Arthur Kan of *Asiaweek* snapped a photograph of the scene (PIC–3). Meantime the television cameras had been catching the movement of a white-shirted security man near the door to the jetway. He seemed to be in charge of the operation and as Lat, deMesa and Aquino came abreast of him he stepped up for a brief word (TV–13).

Just as the long tunnel of the jetway came into view of the television cameras, a fourth soldier in the uniform of the Constabulary (later identified as Moreno) stepped into the airliner cabin. He and a polo baronged security man filed in behind Aquino just before the horde of reporters and cameramen pushed through the door (TV–14 and TV–15). At the moment the "escort" group took its final shape and passed into the jetway, they suddenly swung Aquino to the left, and without warning pulled the Senator through the door leading to the stairway to the ground (TV–16).

Benigno S. Aquino, Jr. was seen by the ABC camera for the last time as he was directed to the doorway 38 seconds after he first started to stand up. He was on the platform as the security man (apparently the one later identified as Miranda) stepped through the doorway (TV–17) at 40 seconds on the NHK timer. TBS also lost sight of Aquino. It began its own timer as the Senator started his descent.

Three seconds into the descent – while the cameramen could hear shouts on the stairway, a khaki-clad soldier pushed in front of the ABC camera to join several security men in the doorway.

TBS was getting the same treatment; five seconds into the descent a security man in the doorway put his hand over the TBS lens (TV–18), knocking the cameraman's hand off the trigger for one second.

There was a tremendous jam at the doorway. Wakamiya was there, jumping up and down to overcome his short stature. Matsumoto was trying to push into position. He would later contend he remembered being in front of Wakamiya, but it is Wakamiya's tousled hair and owlish glasses which keep showing up in the bottom and left hand of the ABC pictures. Reporter Vanzi of UPI and Kashiwahara were desperately trying to see over heads, but could discern nothing. Ueda gave up and was standing in the aisle trying to see out the window from about the third or fourth seat.

While the cameras were effectively blocked off, the high quality microphones encased in sponge rubber were aimed out the doorway. Just as the two-man TBS crew was lifting its camera high enough to see over the security man, (TV–19 and TV–20), the sharp report of a single shot was heard.

A few seconds later there were four more shots – somewhat more distant – in rapid succession. While reporters ran for windows in the jetway or on the plane, the television cameras kept grinding, although they were still being pushed back by the men blocking the door.

Nine and a half seconds after the first shot, ABC got a picture of the security man who had been standing outside on the platform as he began turning to come back through the door (TV–21). Upon close examination, the dark blur on the left turned out to be Wakamiya's hair and one lens of his glasses. Calmly the security man (never identified) took a final look over his shoulder and pushed his way through the door (TV–22 and TV–23).

While photographic journalist Matsumoto tried to push his camera into the opening, Wakamiya had thrown himself on the floor at the doorway after setting his camera. He is seen by ABC at 12 seconds after the first gunshot getting his camera ready.

Less than 20 seconds after Aquino's death shot, he took his first picture (PIC-4). The time could be determined by the fact that the AVSECOM men who fired the final bursts had not yet exited the van. His photo showed a single soldier running away from the location of the van and the two bodies toward the right. Aquino's head and arm could be seen in the left foreground as could the leg and a portion of the body of the alleged killer. An automatic rifle barrel protruded from the door of the van, which is ajar. A man in a polo barong stood peeking out from behind a freight wagon, and with the aid of a magnifying glass, another man could be seen in the same pose looking out from behind the third wagon.

In Wakamiya's next photograph (PIC-5), taken about two seconds later, the soldier was gone, the man behind the first wagon was walking away and the other man had disappeared. While Wakamiya was shooting his second picture, Matsumoto, standing above him, got a broader photo down the stairway (PIC-6).

By approximately 23 seconds after the first shot, Ueda had his camera going. News photographers in the terminal had pushed their way to a window. The van door was now wide open and there was a burst of gunfire at the prone figure of the alleged killer beginning with a shot from a .45 (PIC-7) followed by an M16 burst and random shooting (PIC-8). Ueda commented later: "They were really shooting the guy."

As soon as that firing stopped, one of the soldiers—distinguishable because he wore his cap backwards—put down his weapon and tried to pick up Aquino (PIC-9). There were other soldiers still in the van and two men were deployed on their stomachs in the general direction of the airliner at the next jetway. A second soldier, who lost his cap, helped half drag, half lift Aquino's body (PIC-10). About 50 feet away two uniformed men kept their backs turned. Another view from the jetway showed AVSECOM men with pistols aiming at the plane, while one with his cap on backwards pointed his M16 at the ground (PIC-11).

57

According to the NHK timeclock, Aquino's body was in the van by 32 seconds after his death. The AVSECOM men then climbed in and pulled the door shut. Less than 40 seconds after the first shot the van pulled away, leaving the alleged assailant alone on the ground (PIC–12). The soldier's lost cap lay in Aquino's blood.

The camera crew from TBS had moved to a window in the jetway. Panning around they photographed at least four armed men crouched under the nose of the China airliner (TV–22). Swinging around to a baggage cart, TBS filmed two shadowy figures: one on the left in uniform with a rifle and the other on the right, holding a pistol in his right hand. The quality of the picture was poor, but it seemed that the man in civilian clothes had just picked up a pistol and tucked it under his shirt.

A *Tempo* photographer got a clearer single picture (PIC–13).

Meanwhile, the government camera was again filming (if it actually stopped) and it panned its camera back at the plane. There it spotted a man in a white shirt who came out from behind the jetway pylon and ran toward a car and two men waiting under the edge of the terminal building (TV–27). In the left hand of the man in the white shirt appeared to be Aquino's overnight bag.

Later in the afternoon a photographer took a close-up of the alleged assassin still lying where he had fallen, after the investigation had been made and chalk lines drawn to indicate various locations (PIC–14). The picture was startling – not so much for its gory detail – but because it was obvious that the scene of his death had been disturbed substantially.

In Picture 14 there are two holsters, a pair of glasses which look much like Aquino's (and were confirmed to be so) and at least four unused cartridges between his right hand and his hip. In Picture 5, taken less than 30 seconds after his death, there is only one holster and it is in a different position. There are no bullets and no eyeglasses in that earlier photo. His pants pocket has been turned inside out by Picture 14. In several of the earlier pictures, such as Picture 11, there appears to be a holster approximately four feet away from his right hand. If so, it has now been placed about eight inches away from his right hand.

If the bullets came from his pocket why were they left on the ground next to his hand? Why was the second holster moved to place it next to him? How and why were Aquino's spectacles placed next to the body? And why were they not broken and bloody? Never once in any report, official or media, were the glasses mentioned.

Looking at both pictures, the first taken immediately after his death and the second taken several hours later, the alleged assailant had no identifying badge on his shirt collars or pocket.

The final picture of the dead Galman's face raised another question. If he was shot in the chest and fell backward without any wounds in the face, how did the rivulets of blood on his cheek and forehead run uphill from the wound on the back of his head—contrary to the law of gravity?

Either the death scene was intentionally tampered with for some reason or it displayed investigative ineptitude of the first order.

The actions of more than a dozen security men—in and out of uniform—shown in the vicinity of the death scene defied the normal expectations of human conduct. All of them—except the five or six AVSECOM men who came out shooting after the event—looked away or hid at the first opportunity. Occasionally out of cowardice or confusion a man might duck or run off, but not everyone. In the first place, they were there for one reason: To protect Aquino. If there was trouble they were to halt the assailant. Even if taken by surprise, at the first sound of gunplay the security men were trained to respond. They did not.

Four shots were fired at the alleged killer, but whoever did the shooting then got out of sight. The security agent at the head of the stairway looked on for a moment and then turned into the jetway with only casual concern. Seconds after the second death the only soldier visible ran away while the plainclothesmen behind the freight wagons took a quick look and left. Soldiers beneath the plane's nose scrunched down out of sight. A plainclothesman under the plane with what appears to be Aquino's bag ran to a waiting car after the van pulled out. The two AVSECOM men, who the government claimed were trying to save Aquino's life by putting him in the van, ineptly tossed him about like a side of beef. In the process they destroyed evidence: Placement of bodies, possible bullets and the like. The normal action would have been to call for medics or get a stretcher.

The presence of the two men filmed picking up a pistol could mean almost anything, from clumsiness to culpability. The images are in shadow and do not lend themselves to any conclusion. However, like every other government man in the area they fled the scene.

The actions of the six or seven AVSECOM soldiers who eventually came out of the van were virtually incomprehensible. They waited inside until almost 20 seconds after Aquino was shot. The apparent assassin was probably dead. Then the AVSECOM men went into a 15- to 20-second spate of wild action. Two or three pumped the blue-shirted corpse full of bullets. A couple of soldiers took prone positions in front of the van. Others aimed at the plane and the jetway, and apparently got off a couple of rounds into the air. One man – his cap worn like one of the Little Rascals – aimed his armalite at the ground.

Much like the re-enactment, the men escorting Aquino were nowhere to be seen 20 seconds after Aquino's death when the first picture was taken. They never reappeared. And nowhere did any of the photographs show a murder weapon on the ground.

While men's memories and perceptions may have been imperfect, the cameras in expert hands provided a silent and penetrating story.

(l. to r.) Jim Laurie, ABC; Aquino; Mr. Kagita; Matsuo Ueda, Kyodo News Service; Sandra Burton, Time magazine; Max Vanzi, UPI. Interview during flight to Philippines.

Philippine government videotape of Flight 811 landing.

Soldiers running into place as plane stops. (ABC)

Another soldier running into position. (ABC)

意外に兵士の姿が……

Video from plane shows three men in polo barongs, two in AVSECOM uniforms and one airport security man by terminal as plane shuts down; side stairway at right. (TBS)

Soldier under stairway. (TBS)

AVSECOM van in place (Wakamiya)

Lazaga looking for Aquino, deMesa at left in sunglasses; security agent at background right. (TBS

Lazaga turns back as deMesa finds Aquino; note Lazaga's holster. (TBS)

deMesa covers face when he sees television camera; Lat behind him also has hand to face. (TBS)

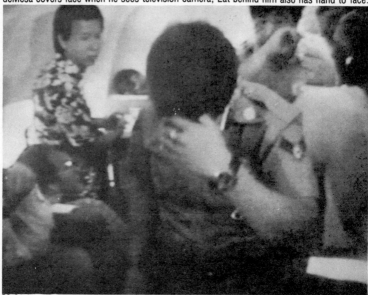

00.01:11 seconds on NHK timeclock which starts when Aquino makes first move to get up; deMesa and Lat are greeting him; Max Vanzi watches. (ABC)

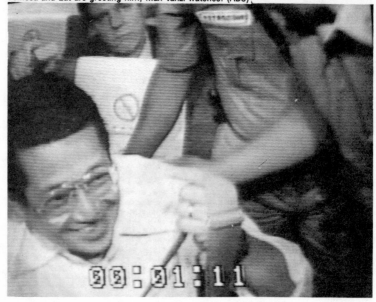

deMesa puts arm around Aquino, feeling for protection according to Vanzi.

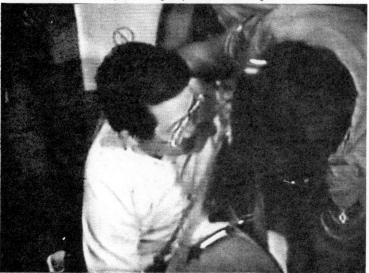

00:03:15 seconds; Aquino gets apprehensive look on face as guards take his bags. (ABC)

00:09:09 seconds; Ken Kashiwahara asks Lazaga if he can accompany Aquino; deMesa says "You just take seat"; photographer Wakamiya looks on. (ABC)

Aquino is held by Lat and deMesa as taken down aisle. —(Arthur Kan, *Asiaweek*).

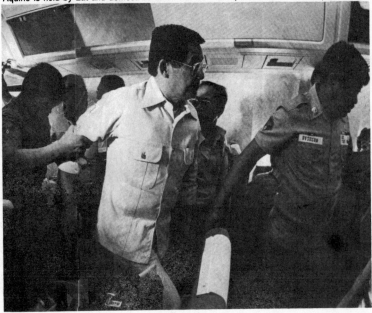

00:29:29 seconds; as uniformed trio reach door to tunnel to terminal, man in polo barong who appears to have been supervising moves in for a brief word. (ABC)

Aquino at left is suddenly turned toward side door as two more plainclothesmen join group: view down jetway to terminal. (TBS)

00:36:25 seconds; another agent steps up; Aquino at left. (ABC)

00:37:24 seconds; Aquino's shoulders in white at left barely visible as soldiers and agents crowd in. (ABC)

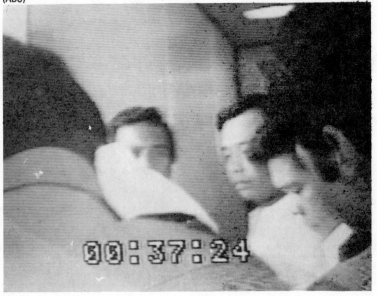

00:40:20 seconds; a man in polo barong stepped in behind Aquino (later identified as Sgt. Miranda) and is framed in doorway; Aquino has taken first step down from platform at this instant. (ABC)

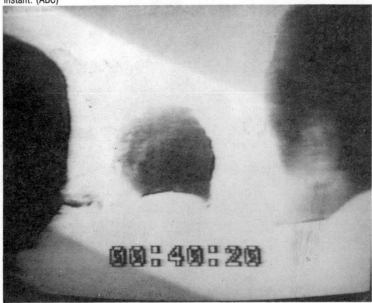

TBS put timer on as Aquino stepped down out of view; 05:6 seconds into descent, one of agents in doorway pushed his hand over TBS camera lens. (TBS)

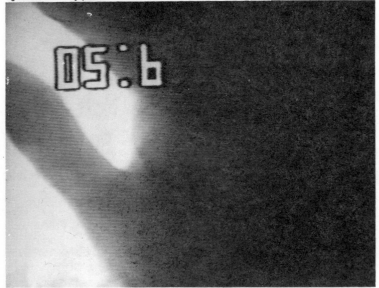

Back of agent's head in doorway, two-tenths of a second before first shot. (TBS)

00:52:08 seconds, three seconds after first shot; ABC camera shows TBS cameraman lifting camera over crowd. (ABC)

00:58:11 seconds, five seconds after first shots at Galman; plainclothesman who has been on platform looking back over shoulder as he starts to re-enter door; Wakamiya's head at lower left. (ABC)

00:59:06 seconds — plainclothesmen starting to move through door; Wakamiya's glasses show at left. (ABC)

01:01:08 seconds — agent enters with soldier seen below on tarmac; final shots at Galman have not yet occurred. (ABC)

PIC-4: Wakamiya photo between legs of people in doorway; taken about 20 seconds after Aquino's death; a soldier runs away from the bodies which are at foreground left; two men in polo barongs are behind the first and third baggage trucks; the muzzle of an M16 protrudes from the partially open door of the van.

PIC-5: Another Wakamiya photo a couple of seconds later with soldier gone and man behind first truck walking away.

74

PIC-6: Matsumoto photo from doorway to stairs, approximately a second later, which shows a television microphone, the van door swinging open, and a uniformed man walking casually in middle distance.

PIC-7: A reporter in the terminal got to a window and took this picture approximately 25 seconds after Aquino's death, showing hand aiming .45 at Galman; only one holster shows and no bullets are on ground — Ben Mulamay/*Peoples Journal*

PIC-8: From inside the plane at approximately 27 seconds after Aquino's death, showing the soldiers

PIC-9: Taken from a window in the jetway, photo shows one of soldiers has put down his weapon and is trying to lift Aquino

78

PIC-10: Two soldiers lift Aquino's body as one loses his cap; note the uniformed men in the background looking away— (Ueda)

PIC-11: Same scene with soldiers pointing guns at plane and jetway.

80

TV-24: At 01:20:11 on NHK timer (31 seconds after first shot) Aquino thrown into van. (ABC)

TV-25: As the van pulls away 36 seconds after Aquino's death, an agent in doorway puts hand over ABC lens.

PIC-12: Galman is left on the tarmac; note holster about four or five feet to his right. (Ueda)

TV-26: After the van pulls out, ABC picks up at least four people huddled under the nose of the plane.

TV-27: The government videotape begins again after van pulls away and spots a man running from under the jetway to a waiting car; he is later identified as Sgt. Miranda.

PIC-13: *Tempo* and television both spotted this man with pistol by baggage cart. (Louie Perez/*Tempo*)

J-1: Layout of Manila International Airport shown on Japanese television.

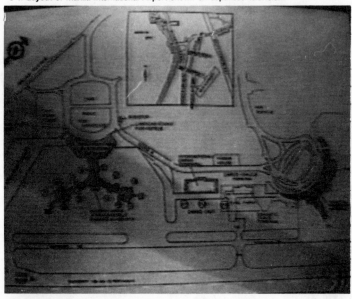

J-2: Announcer demonstrates theory of downward trajectory; shows position of shooter if on level with Aquino.

J-3: Detective shows how shot that killed Aquino would have come from stairs with downward trajectory.

J-4: A typical police holster shown on Japanese television.

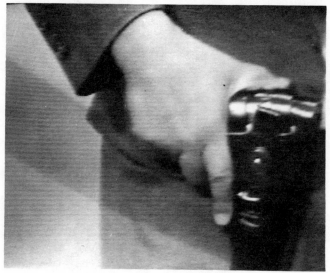

J-5: Sonogram of first shots from soundtrack; first dark line on left is shot that killed Aquino, three at right were shots at Galman, beginning 3.5 seconds later.

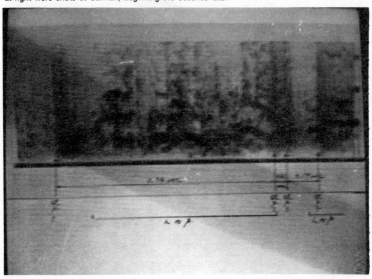

J-6: Dr. Matsumi Suzuki at press conference in which he explains voice patters from sound track. Kiyoshi Wakayima holds board.

CHAPTER 9

Hard Evidence: Sound and Fury

Although the security agents were able to block the TBS and ABC television cameras from filming the crucial fourteen seconds of the morbid drama, the audio microphones were operating throughout. It is a credit to the sophistication of the equipment as well as to the men handling it that so much quality sound recording is available.

As it turned out, there were several elements of evidence provided by these tapes. They established unequivocally the time sequence of shots in relation to Aquino's descent from the plane in the hands of his reception squad. Secondly, they provided information as to the differing distances from the plane of the first fatal shot and the subsequent gunfire. Finally, the equipment was sensitive enough to pick up the words of the guards during the fatal trip to the tarmac.

The ABC camera lost sight of Aquino at 11 seconds prior to the fatal shot, but the TBS camera still had a glimpse of him. Based on the TBS videotape the time from the beginning of descent to the sound of the first shot was 9.2 seconds. It was necessary to match the sounds on both the TBS and ABC audios to confirm this time since a second was lost by the TBS camera because the cameraman's finger slipped from the trigger when his camera lens was pushed by a security man.

89

The accompanying chart shows the proven time sequence of all shots fired. By the time the last burst was fired there were visual opportunities.

Of equal importance to the time from start of descent to Aquino's death shot, is the time gap before the second shot is fired. The time is 3.5 seconds between the first and a volley of four shots, and it is assumed that this volley struck the alleged assassin.

According to visual evidence and eyewitnesses, before the final volley the man in blue denims is on his back, dead or dying. The gap in time from the first group of four that felled him until the final burst of 12 to 14 shots is just under 20 seconds. The first of these by the picture evidence was the shot by the AVSECOM man firing his .45 from the door of the van, followed by other AVSECOM men shooting their M16 armalites repeatedly at the dead body of Galman.

NHK had a sonogram made of the sound of gunfire. On the sonogram the first shot appeared as a sharp black line which showed that it was relatively close to the sound equipment aimed at Aquino from the door of the stairway. The other shots were dimmer and the lines were hazier. Listening to the tapes one gets the same impression. A gray line immediately after the initial death shot was the echo off the MIA terminal building. The experts for NHK could not determine the type of gun which fired the initial shot, based on the sound.

Amazingly, both the TBS and the ABC microphones were sufficiently well aimed to pick up the voices of the escorts as they descended the stairs. The words are in a Filipino dialect.

The TBS sound track recorded the following between 43 seconds and 48 seconds after Aquino left his seat (40 seconds being the start of the descent and 49 seconds being the first shot):

"*Akona*" which means "let me do it" or "I'll do it"

"*Akona*" in a different voice

"*Op*" which is idiomatic for "oh"

"*Eto na*" which means "here he is"

"*Ya*" which has no special meaning, but may be slang for "yeah"

"*Op*" another "oh"

"*Pusila*" "Shoot" or "Shoot him"

"*Pusila*" repeated in a different voice at almost 48 seconds — one second before the death shot.

Dr. Matsumi Suzuki, Director of the Japanese Acoustic Laboratories, at the request of the magazine *Shukan Sankei* (for which reporter Wakamiya is a columnist) studied a voice print from the TBS tape. He discovered that the AVSECOM man who told Ken Kashiwahara, "You just take seat" was also the man to call out "Akona" ("I'll do it") on the stairs. Dr. Suzuki, the same analyst who pieced together the radio messages surrounding the Russians' downing of the Korean airliner, separated out four men talking on the stairs. They are identified as A through D on the voiceprint in Figure 5. While in the final analysis who spoke which words is not crucial — but rather that they were said. There are clues to the identity of the speakers which may help clarify what happened on the stairway.

"A," the AVSECOM man who told Kashiwahara to sit down, is later identified as Sergeant deMesa, who was holding Aquino on the left side going down the staircase. "C" appears to be in command with the "Here he comes" statement as well as the first "Shoot him." "B" seems always to respond to others, but he echoes the "Shoot him." Thus, if one of those speaking did any shooting it would not be "C" or "B" since both are ordering the shooting.

This leaves it to "A" (deMesa) or "D" who is unknown. Both of them offered to do something at the start of the trip down in saying "Let me do it" or "I'll do it." Of course, "I'll do it" could refer to almost anythng and not just murder. One factor of interest, however, reported by Dr. Suzuki is that "A's" voice, although matching the voice pattern of deMesa in the plane when

91

he said "You just take seat" on all 10 voice qualities, was higher pitched when he said "I'll do it," indicating tension or excitement.

When the government finally revealed the names of the men who accompanied Aquino down the stairway, holding him were Sergeant Arnulfo deMesa ("A") on his left and Sergeant Claro Lat on his right (Lat appeared in the video and still pictures as the man pulling Aquino by the wrist down the aisle of the plane). Behind them was Constabularyman Rogelio Moreno. Next was a new character in the scenario, Technical Sergeant Filomeno Miranda, a plainclothes security man, who the government revealed was "Team Leader." Behind trailed Constabularyman Mario Lazaga. Not mentioned in the government's reports was a second security man who stood at the top of the stairs. Lieutenant Jesus Castro remained inside the door to the stairs.

Since Miranda was the team leader he was the likely one to give orders and thus was probably "C." That makes Moreno, who was in front of Miranda, a likely candidate to be "B," the man who repeated the "Shoot him" directive. Lazaga, trailing behind, was probably the silent one. This left Sergeant Lat, who seemed to argue over who would "do it" at Aquino's right side as "D." However, the order to shoot (voice "C") may have come from someone waiting on the ground. That would be a possibility since "C" also said "Here he is."

The videotapes reveal the voices were raucous and the speakers seemed to be bunched together, apparently ruling out the possibility that the voices came from anyone other than the group on the stairs or someone at the foot of the stairway.

Any idea that the "Shoot him" orders were directed toward Galman is ruled out by the fact that they came before the shooting of Aquino and all accounts, including the government's, do not put Galman into view until after the shot through Aquino's head.

The fainter lines on the NHK sonogram indicate that the later shots killing Galman originated from a greater distance from the cameras than did the one that killed Aquino.

As it would turn out, the sounds of gunfire would prove to

be hard evidence of the most valuable sort in piecing together what happened – or did not occur – during the 30 seconds that the media eyes were effectively frustrated.

The exact reason the various words were spoken and whether they were directed to others than those in the escort group can only be surmised. However, the phrases are truly significant in that they do not appear in any official version of the case, nor do they make any sense (except possibly "Here he is") in the context of the government's version of the killing.

Time Sequence

0:00:0 Aquino on platform, starting down.

0:05:6 Agent put hand over TBS camera lens.

0:08:0 Second cry of "pusila".

0:09:2 Sound of single shot, close.

0:12:0 TBS tried to lift camera to get view.

0:12:3 Start of four shots lasting just over one half second, farther away.

0:21:3 Agent on platform came in with last look over shoulder; one soldier on tarmac in view.

0:23:0 Approximate time of Wakamiya's first photo of scene; both men lying on tarmac; one soldier running to right; two agents peeking out from back of luggage trucks.

0:24:0 Approximate time of second Wakamiya picture; agent behind truck, walking away.

0:24:2 Approximate time of Matsumoto picture down stairway; van doors opening, but no one out.

0:25:0 Approximate time of first movement out of van.

0:28:0 Approximate time of beginning of prolonged gunfire; first Ueda picture and first local news photos.

0:29:0 Approximate time when soldier began trying to lift Aquino's body; gunfire still going on.

0:31:3 Exact time Aquino's body put in van.

0:36:0 Van pulled out.

0:40:0 Approximate time Sgt. Miranda ran from hiding place to waiting auto.

REPUBLIC OF THE PHILIPPINES
MINISTRY OF JUSTICE
NATIONAL BUREAU OF INVESTIGATION
MEDICO-LEGAL DIVISION
MANILA

AUTOPSY REPORT NO. N-83-2236...

Decedant ....BENIGNO S. AQUINO, JR....   Male   50yrs.   Male   Male   Filipino
    Name   Civil Status   Age   Sex   Race   Nationality

....Married   ....Former Senator....   25 Times St., Quezon City
Civil Status   Occupation   Address   277, Boulevard Ave., No. 18,
                                                    Pasig City, Rizal
Identified by Lupita Aquino Kashiwahara....   Sister
Dead on arrival at Station Hospital, Fort Bonifacio   Makati to Deceased
....Bonifacio, Makati, Metro Manila   Manila Manila   August 21, 1983
                Place   Day & Time
Allegedly resulting from ...Shooting....   Airport, Manila   August 21, 1983
                                        Place   Day & Time
Autopsied at LOYOLA Mem. Chapel Morgue August 21,1983 at 10:30PM 169.0cm.
                Place   Date & Time   Length   Weight
Requesting Officer or party Gen. Prospero Olivas, Commanding Officer, Metrocom

POSTMORTEM FINDINGS

Pallor, conjunctivae and integument, marked and generalized.

Abrasion, reddish brown, lower eyelid, right, 1.5 x 2.0 cm.

Contusions, dark blue; upper eyelid, right, 1.5 x 1.7 cm.; upper eyelid,
left, 2.0 x 2.8 cm.; upper lip, across midline, 1.9 x 7.0 cm.; lip, lower
mucosa, left side; left shoulder, left, anterior, 0.2 x 0.3 cm.; arm, left, upper
3rd. anterior, two in number, each measuring 0.2 x 0.3 cm.

Pinpoint hemorrhages, multiple; forehead, left side, anterior aspect,
disparsed over an area 7.5 x 8.0 cm.; cheek, left, disparsed over an area
2.5 x 6.5 cm.

Hematoma, scalp, parietal region, left, 6.0 x 7.5 cm.

Contused abrasion, forehead, right side, 1.5 x 5.6 cm.

94

by a contusion collar widest at its superior border, with an area of tattooing, 3.0 x 6.0 cm., more at its anterior border; located at the mastoid region, left, 5.1 cm. behind and 2.5 cm. below external auditory meatus, 157.0 cm. above left heel; directed forward, downward and medially, fracturing comminutedly the occipital bone, left side, with linear extensions into the left temporal bone, left parietal bone, occipital bone, right side, into the cranial cavity, lacerating the occipital lobe, left, and cerebellum, fracturing the right temporal bone, where a metallic fragment was embedded and extracted, then fracturing the petrous portion of left temporal bone, mandible and finally making an exit wound, irregular in shape, anterior portion, mandible, 1.5 x 0.8 cm., 149.5 cm. above right heel, surrounded by an area of contused abrasion 3.0 x 3.5 cm.; two metallic fragments recovered at the wound of exit.

Hemorrhage, intracranial, massive, generalized.

Laceration, brain, extensive.

Heart, covered with adipose tissue, apex adherent to dome of diaphragm; presence of triple coronary bypass involving anterior descending branch of left coronary artery, left circumflex and right coronary.

Other visceral organs, pale.

~~Stomach~~ Stomach, empty.

* * * * *

CAUSE OF DEATH: Brain laceration and intracranial hemorrhage secondary to gunshot wound of the head.

* * * * *

REMARKS: Three (3) pieces of metallic fragments recovered; submitted to Firearms Investigation Section, NBI for ballistics examination.

Linear scar, running along mid-sternal line, anterior aspect, chest.

* * * * *

Submitted by:

BIENVENIDO O. MUÑOZ, M.D.
— MEDICO-LEGAL OFFICER —

110.05L—p.40427

/arp

APPROVED & NOTED:

PEDRO P. SOLIS
Deputy Director, Technical Services

Fig. 3a. Aquino Autopsy Report, Page 1.

95

Fig. 3b. Aquino Autopsy, Page 2.

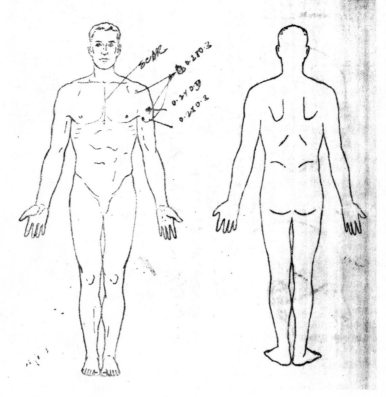

MEDICO LEGAL DIVISION
N B I

Name *Benigno Aquino*　　　　　　Number *N-83-2226*

Address　　　　　　　　　　　　　Height

Medico-Legal Officer *Dr. Bienvenido O. Muñoz*　Weight

Autopsied At　　　　　　　　　　　Nationality

Date & Time of Autopsy *Aug. 21, 1983 10:00 pm*　Photo By :

Requesting Officer　　　　　　　　Mortician

96

Fig. 3c. Aquino Autopsy, Page 3.

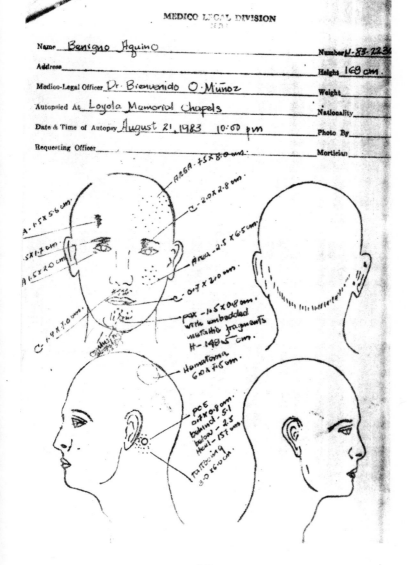

MEDICO LEGAL DIVISION

Name Benigno Aquino

Number N-83-2234

Address

Height 168 cm

Medico-Legal Officer Dr. Brenvenido O. Muñoz

Weight

Autopsied At Loyola Memorial Chapels

Nationality

Date & Time of Autopsy August 21, 1983 10:00 pm

Photo By

Requesting Officer

Mortician

Fig. 4. Galman Autopsy Report Printout.

```
   518            K                        202151                    (1 KEW
AUTOPSY OF ALLEGED AQUINO ASSASSIN

   UKKNOWN ADULT MALE, 30-35 YRS OLD AUTOPSIED AT PC CRIME LAB AUG 21 AT 11:30
P.M.
HEIGHT- 175 CM
WOUNDS - 1: 6.5 CM BEHIND AND 2.0 CM ABOVE LEFT EXTERNAL AUDITORY
MEATUS...PENETRATING CRANIAL CAVITY (BEHIND LEFT EAR)
         2: ...PENETRATING LEFT THORACIC CAVITY (CHEST FRONT)
         3: ...LEFT LATERAL ASPECT OF CHEST (LEFT FRONT CHEST)
         4. ...LEFT HYPHOCHONDRIAC REGION LEVEL OF COSTAL ARCH
         5. ...LOCATED AT BACK, INFERIOR BORDER OF THE INTERSCAPULAR SPACE
            (BACK OF CHEST)
         6: ...LOCATED AT BACK, LEFT INFRASCAPULAR REGION ----
         7: ...NINE IN NUMBER, LARGEST 0.9 X 0.7 CM AND SMALLEST 0.6 X 0.5
            CM...LOCATED OVER AN AREA OF 27 X 3  CM FROM HYPOGASTRIC REGION
            DOWN TO RIGHT THIGH DIRECTED BACKWARD AND UPWARD (HIT BY BULLET
            FROM FRONT POSSIBLY FROM PRONE SHOOTER AND ONE BULLET CAUSED ALL
            THE NINE PUNCTURES ON STOMACH DOWN TO THIGH)
         8. ...LOCATED AT ELBOW REGION.

GRAZING WOUNDS, NUMBERING TWO
SCARS, NUMBERING TWO, 1.5 X 1.0 CM AND 1.0 BY 1.0 CM EACH AT RIGHT AND LEFT
EXTERNAL CANTHI (OF BOTH EYES- THIS IS VERY VAGUE)
SCAR: 8.0 CM LENGTH, RIGHT THIGH LOWER 3RD
SCAR, NUMBERING TWO, 8.0 AND 5.0 CM AT RIGHT SHIN UPPER 3RD
STOMACH IS FILLED UP TO 1/3 WITH PARTIALLY DIGESTED RICE.

CAUSE OF DEATH: SHOCK SECONDARY TO MULTIPLE GUNSHOT WOUNDS
REMARKS: FOUR DEFORMED JACKETED BULLETS, ONE DEFORMED COPPER JACKET AND TWO
SLIGHTLY DEFORMED JACKETED BULLETS RECOVERED AND SUBMITTED TO
INVESTIGATION SECTION, NBI.

   D: NIETO M. SALVADOR, M.D.; MEDICO-LEGAL OFFICER
   PROVED: PEDRO P. SOLIS, DEPUTY DIRECTOR, TECHNICAL SERVICES  NBI
```

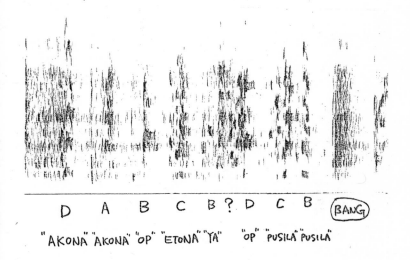

Fig. 5. Sonogram of Voices on Stairway.

CHAPTER 10

Softer Evidence: The Eyewitnesses

Perhaps the most unusual aspect of the Aquino case is the absence of comprehensive eyewitness testimony. There were over 100 arriving passengers on China Airlines Flight 811. On board and on the ground was the Chinese airline crew. By the government's count there were over 1,000 security and military men at the airport, including approximately 70 in the immediate area. In the terminal and beyond were 20,000 friends and supporters of Aquino. Gathered at the entrance to Gate 8 in the main terminal were reporters, and cameramen.Within the term inal was an official television camera and on towers, automa tic surveillance cameras.

This was a double shooting in broad daylight in a public place. Eventually the government would come up with six "witnesses" whose stories turned out to be partial at best and often devoid of detail. But they were all participants and not independent witnesses.

One passenger on the China Airlines flight was interviewed by newsmen on the afternoon after the killing, but the government did not think it was worthwhile questioning him. His is the only recorded statement by anyone who was not either a participant in guarding Aquino or one of Aquino's group on the plane. His name: Hartmut Albath, a passenger from West Germany.

The Philippines Daily Express reported the interview with Albath as follows:

> A West German passenger who was on the China Airlines flight that brought in former Sen. Benigno Aquino, Jr. yesterday has one of the best eyewitness accounts on how Aquino was shot.
>
> The passenger, Hartmut Albath, said he recognized Aquino from the attention given to him on the China Airlines flight from Taipei.
>
> He said Aquino was being escorted down the plane's steps by an armed guard "when I saw him fall down and at the same time a uniformed man shot another man in blue jeans and blue shirt and he fell down also."
>
> Albath told Reuters that after Aquino fell, "I saw blood coming out very much from the left side of his neck . . .
>
> "He was lying on his face on the tarmac. There was so much blood coming out of him like a fountain."
>
> He said four or five uniformed men boarded the plane when it landed at Manila and escorted Aquino from it.
>
> He said Aquino was being led to an airport security van, held by the elbow, when he pitched forward on the airport apron just as his guards opened the vehicle door.
>
> Albath said as Aquino's body was lifted into the van, one of the guards reappeared from the vehicle and evidently emptied his automatic rifle into the body of the man in jeans.

There is one apparent internal inconsistency in the Albath story as reported. At first he said that Aquino fell down as he was being escorted down the plane's steps. Later on the reporter wrote that Aquino pitched forward while being led to the security van just as his guards opened the vehicle door. Eliminate the word "his" just before "guards" and the newspaper line would read: ". . . . he pitched forward just as guards opened the vehicle door."

As filtered through the newsman, Albath sounded uncertain as to whether Aquino pitched forward from the steps or as he was being led to the van. Both could be true since from the moment he started down the stairway he was being led to the van. Thus, the exact location cannot be determined by the news story. However, the article places Aquino on the stairs when Albath is directly quoted.

Albath stated that the man in the jeans was seen by him "at the same time" and shot by a "uniformed man."

It is what Albath did not say that is most significant. He obviously saw what happened from the moment Aquino fell down until the final burst of gunfire. Never once did he report that the man in jeans had a gun, or that he was spun around and fell on his back, or that he came from behind Aquino and his guards.

The West German's spontaneous comments on what he saw are not conclusive that the government's version is untrue, but the Albath statement is inconsistent with the official story.

While the other journalists jammed the area around the door to the side staircase, reporter Ueda of Kyoto News Agency stood somewhere between the third and sixth windows on the left side of the plane facing the tarmac. In an interview with NHK television within a week of the shooting, Mr. Ueda reported:

"I was trying to look out through the window when I heard the first shot. I was really shocked and looked out. I saw Senator Aquino on the ground. The impression is that that was the moment he fell down."

Question: "You did not see the actual moment of the shooting?"

"No, I didn't."

Question: "Did you see the man in the blue shirt?"

"Yes. I saw him standing there as if he had been at a loss. Then I saw two men with guns. There were more shots and this man also fell down."

In a TBS interview he commented: "I saw a man standing on the left. If this man was the assassin why was he facing Senator Aquino?"

This is not so much a question as a statement. Ueda, who

comes off as a calm, dispassionate witness, has placed the alleged assassin in front of Aquino "at a loss" instead of coming around from behind to shoot Aquino as in the official version.

A less dispassionate witness is the energetic Kiyoshi Wakamiya, the young reporter-photographer, who got the first known photograph of the murder scene after the shooting.

Wakamiya was widely quoted around the world for saying that Aquino was shot by two guards who were accompanying him. Apparently, when the soldier emptied his automatic rifle into the alleged assailant's body, he yelled out that the soldiers were shooting Aquino again, which was obviously incorrect.

The threshhold problem with Wakamiya was that on occasion he mixed together what he saw with surmise and opinion. Typical was his interview with ABC-NHK shortly after returning to Japan the same week: "As they [Aquino and the guards] were going down, these two people pulled out their guns – I think a .45 caliber. You see, Mr. Aquino had a bullet-proof vest. Bang. Bang. Then, Mr. Aquino fell forward. Then, this man got out of this vehicle unsteadily and the same man who shot Mr. Aquino shot him two or three times in the stomach. Then this man probably got on to his vehicle because he was gone in an instant. Everything happened so fast."

He also referred to himself as an "eyewitness," but to what?

When pressed by reporters, he said that he did not actually see the pistols, but saw the guards reach for them. He was merely guessing that they would be .45's. His partial recanting of the suppositions and overstatement was picked up by Reuters and used by the government to discredit his entire story.

At the Foreign Correspondents Club in Tokyo on September 6, Wakamiya made the following statement:

After Senator Aquino reached the ground and took one or two steps, the two uniformed guards accompanying him on his left made movements as if they were drawing their guns. (I did not see the firearms themselves.)

"What's going on?" I thought. At that moment, a shot

104

rang out, and Senator Aquino fell forward like a log onto the runway. Blood spurted from his head, his face turned to his left. My instant reaction was that he had been killed; I was certain he was dead.

An AVSECOM van was parked on the runway. Out of the left corner of my field of vision, from the van or close thereto, a man staggered forward as if he had been pushed from behind by someone. He did not have a gun.

Soon thereafter, from the right side of my field of vision, several soldiers appeared and shot at the man. I believe they were using rifles. The man took three or four shots to his stomach and fell to the ground on his back.

The guards who had escorted Senator Aquino from the airplane could not be seen at this time. I immediately fell on my stomach and started to take several photographs with my camera . . .

Excluding his speculation, Wakamiya clings to four essentials:

1. That the guards reached as if they were going to draw guns.

2. Aquino fell forward just beyond the foot of the stairs.

3. The alleged assassin was in front of Aquino in the staggering posture and without a gun.

4. The man was shot while still standing up.

To help judge his credibility it is worth tracing his movements during the crucial seconds. He first shows up on the videotape (TV–12) with his distinctive moustache and beard standing behind Ken Kashiwahara when deMesa is telling the brother-in-law to take a seat. Short in stature, the back of Wakamiya's tousled head was seen bouncing up and down in front of the ABC camera during Aquino's descent down the stairway. Therefore, he was in position possibly to see something.

The ABC videotape showed him adjusting his camera at 11 seconds after Aquino was shot, and he reported he then dropped to the floor. This was confirmed by the fact that his last three of five pictures in the series are of pants legs and shoes.

Wakamiya's corrections in his story would cause him great problems if cross-examined in court, but the four key elements of his narrative upon which he insists, are consistent with Ueda's observations and not in conflict with Albath's. Thus, together with the other eye-witnesses his story has some "make weight" value.

There are a host of rumors – some from people who have reliable credentials – that there are several witnesses among the China airliner passengers and at least one man who got to a window in the terminal who claimed that one of the escorts shot Aquino and that the alleged assassin first appeared in front of the Senator. For purposes of serious analysis these cannot be given any consideration.

Paul Quinn-Judge, Manila correspondent for the *Christian Science Monitor*, reported on November 18 that two officers "with intimate knowledge" of military intelligence operations claimed to have interviewed witnesses who said that Aquino was shot by one of the guards. Although legitimate reportage, without the names and basis of knowledge of such witnesses, such comments were outside the realm of acceptable evidence. They were not only the usually banned hearsay evidence, but they were actually hearsay on hearsay.

Until late November, the testimony of the six government "eyewitnesses" was also of the hearsay variety since their stories were told by General Olivas on their behalf.

CHAPTER 11

Ballistics and Bouncing Bullets

Metrocom chief Major General Prospero Olivas announced five days after the killing that he had received the findings of a National Bureau of Investigation ballistics report "conducted on pieces of lead fragments found inside the body of Aquino." The autopsy had referred to three such fragments.

Although the first reports from the scene had not included a spent .357 bullet, but only armalite and .45 shells, Olivas had later said that such a bullet had been found on the tarmac. *Bulletin Today*, August 27, quoted Olivas:

> "The deformed copper jacket and the fired shell's caliber showed they were fired from the death weapon, the .357 Smith & Wesson caliber revolver."

All that said was that the loose deformed jacket came from the Smith & Wesson in the government's possession. It did not prove it to be the death weapon.

Olivas continued:

> "The ballistics finding revealed that the submitted evidence possesses similar individual characteristic markings with the test bullets and test shells fired from the revolver, showing these were fired from this particular firearm, according to the NBI report."

It was difficult to conceive how the three metallic fragments could have been compared to a test bullet to match "individual characteristic markings" which are caused by the minute riflings in the barrel and are transmitted to the bullet during its brief passage from chamber to thin air.

When the actual ballistics report was released about a month later it turned out it said no such thing. Instead of claiming "characteristic markings" the report said: "A lead fragment of a bullet extracted from the head of the Ex-Senator by the NBI medico-legal officer, Dr. Bienvenido O. Munoz. . .had similar *constituents* as the lead core of the Magnum bullet. . ." In short, both were lead. In December, the NBI confirmed that the fragments were so small they could not prove what type of bullet they came from.

The autopsy report had shown a bullet entry and exit which created a downward trajectory of approximately 22 degrees. Dr. Munoz had used the term "downward" in his report made the night of the killing. He had also noted a pattern of powder burns which the government said indicated a distance of not more than 18 inches from muzzle to the back of Aquino's head.

A hole about 0.8 centimeters in diameter was made at point of entry in the neck and there was an exit wound less than double that size in the chin. As part of its special on the Aquino assassination, Tokyo Broadcasting System presented a Japanese policeman, Detective Kunimoto. Displaying two bullets, Kunimoto said: "This is a .357 magnum like the alleged weapon, and this is a .357 cartridge. Unlike an ordinary cartridge, as you can see here, the lead is exposed and when it hits an object, the lead breaks and scatters into pieces causing extensive damage. If the bullet hole of the entry wound is 8–9 mm in diameter as reported by the Philippine police, then we would expect that half of his lower face would have been blown off."

Law enforcement people who were questioned agreed in general with Kunimoto. However, one pathologist pointed out that if the .357 shell lost a good deal of its body during its traverse of the head it could leave a smaller hole than the one suggested by Kunimoto. Nevertheless, chances were that the .357 magnum, the second most powerful pistol in the world (the .44 magnum has a heavier bullet), would have done more extensive damage to Aquino's face. Dr. Munoz's autopsy reported that the bits of bullet left in the skull were fragmentary, and in December the NBI confirmed this.

Detective Kunimoto also discussed the matter of trajectory in relation to the hand holding the murder weapon. (J-1). He assumed, as the television pictures show, that the 22 degree downward trajectory was more or less constant. His thesis was that, no matter what the relative heights of shooter and victim, the shot had to be from an elevated position. If the killer were at the same level as Aquino, as the official version ran, then the normal shot would have been in the back and the trajectory would have been at least 25 degrees upward. The human wrist and shoulder are not constructed so as to raise the revolver high enough to shoot downward into the neck. On the other hand, if the shooter were standing on the same level as the victim and shot him in the back, the pistol would have been pointed decidedly upward.

Picture J-1 illustrated the impossible awkwardness of the downward shot and Picture J-2 showed the commentator demonstrating how Kunimoto figured the death blow was delivered from a position on the stairway.

Among those doubting the government's story, there had been considerable debate as to the relative heights of Aquino and the alleged assassin. Apparent inaccuracies and changes in reporting the heights of the two men added fuel to the rhetorical fire. Ninoy Aquino was well known to be somewhere between five feet nine and ten inches (the extra inch possibly due to thick heels), but the official autopsy measured him at only five feet six inches. The suspected killer was first reported by General Olivas to be five feet five and then five feet seven, but the NBI autopsy measured him out at five feet ten inches. The suspicion was that the autopsy had been doctored to meet the claim that the assassin had to be taller.

As explained by two pathologists, when an autopsy is performed, height is not a major consideration and is sometimes determined quickly based on markings on the work table or by approximation. Therefore, the discrepancies may have no nefarious significance. In any event, height differences have no bearing on the position of the shooter to Aquino.

On September 6, the opening day of the official commission's hearings on the Aquino murder, Dr. Munoz was the principal witness. Aided by an old skull for demonstrative evidence, he testified that it was "improbable" that Aquino had been shot from above. He said that either Ninoy had been looking up or the bullet had been deflected by the skull with sufficient force to change direction.

The commission's assistant attorney, Amadeo Seno, asked Dr. Munoz: "Assuming he was standing up, what was the bullet's trajectory?"

"Forward and downward," Munoz answered, but he continued, the bullet was deflected by bone and "did not travel in a straight line."

Seno asked: "Could we say the gun was pointed downward?"

"No, no, only the bullet's trajectory was downward."

In response to a further question, Dr. Munoz contended that the bullet would have followed the same tumbling path even if Aquino's head were tilted forward. Counsel Seno did not follow up on this apparent contradiction.

San Francisco Examiner Reporter Phil Bronstein reported that Seno said afterward: "I am confused by the testimony." Asked why he did not inquire of Munoz if he had been coached before the testimony since it seemed in contradiction to the autopsy, Seno told Bronstein: "I don't want to go back to the stockade," since he had been jailed twice during the martial law period.

Even under the limited examination, Munoz admitted he had "very superficial" knowledge of ballistics and knew "nothing about guns." Nevertheless he stuck by his bouncing bullet theory while Seno approached the question several ways. Bronstein's story concluded with Seno's admission that Munoz's testimony defied common sense, but "I tried but he insisted. I cannot wring his neck."

The idea – alluded to by Dr. Munoz – that Aquino might have been looking up, ran contrary to usual human experience. When a man is being escorted along unfamiliar ground, particularly down a metal stairway, without being able to hold the bannister, his natural act would be to look down for safe footing. In any event, if he looked up, without external pressure the neck could not bend back sufficiently to account for 22 degrees of downward trajectory.

A veteran pathologist stated that a bullet could certainly change course when it encountered bone and could follow an erratic or unexpected tumbling path. He pointed out that one problem in determining trajectory was that brain tissue is soft and does not always leave a clear path to follow. Therefore, Dr. Munoz's theory was at least within the range of possibility.

What was particularly strange about his testimony before the commission three weeks after the autopsy was his absolute certainty that the bullet entered in a trajectory that was not downward, but then started downward only after hitting bone. Attorney Seno, afraid of the stockade or not, pursued the matter and could not shake him.

Such a divergence from the expected trajectory is a possibility, but could not be stated as a certainty. Why Dr. Munoz expressed one possible alternative in that fashion, particularly after he had originally used the words "directed forward, downward and medially" to describe the bullet's path, can only be a matter of speculation.

An experienced pathologist informed the authors that the Autopsy Report presented by Dr. Munoz – particularly involving murder of a prominent person – was sketchy in form; in the United States the protocol would require inclusion of dictated notes, possibly greater detail, and photos.

A gunshot wound to the head from a gun of major caliber often creates an egg-shell explosion effect on the skull and brain causing death, even though the bullet does not directly kill by piercing the brain. This generalized condition makes flat out statements of individual trajectory often impossible.

General Olivas had announced in the first week of the investigation that Sergeant deMesa – the guard on Aquino's left – had recovered the .357 Smith & Wesson revolver from the gunman. In turn he had passed it on to another AVSECOM man, later to be identified as Master Sergeant Martinez, who eventually gave it to General Custodio, who held it up at the airport press conference the day of the killing. Oddly enough, the reenactment did not show the man playing deMesa go near the fallen assassin.

The alleged assassin was fired on four times between 3 to 4.0 seconds after Aquino was shot. There are approximately ten seconds thereafter in which deMesa could have scrambled to his feet and run over, taken the revolver and hidden behind the van without being in the way of fellow AVSECOM men shooting or being seen by either television or news cameras.

Possibly in response to the published reports of journalist Wakamiya's claim that the guards shot Senator Aquino within a few days after the assassination, General Olivas announced that the men escorting Aquino were unarmed.

Pro-government newspapers carried a report in the second week that the Japanese videotapes showed no holsters on the escorts. What the newspapers were referring to was a brief film clip of Aquino being greeted by Lat and deMesa. In reality the full videotapes showed holsters on Lazaga and Moreno, but whether they contained pistols could not be determined.

Olivas had also announced the first week that some 14 of the "close-in" AVSECOM security men had been subjected to paraffin tests by the National Bureau of Investigation, apparently to determine who had fired weapons. He promptly reported that the test was "positive" on both hands of the dead assassin, but as it turned out the results on the AVSECOM men would not come out for several weeks and then almost by accident.

Whether the doubters who believed that Kunimoto was right about the shot that killed Aquino coming from some elevation, or those who chose Dr. Munoz's recently-discovered theory of the bouncing bullet, the debate had been joined. While tens of thousands honored Benigno S. Aquino, Jr. at various rallies, copies of the Japanese videotapes began finding their way into the Philippines, some disguised as Playboy movies.

Rumor, speculation and invective could not shake the government's version despite the mysterious circumstances surrounding Ninoy Aquino's death.

CHAPTER 12

The Smoking Gun

During the American political trauma known as Watergate, there were many references to "The Smoking Gun." The investigators had to find "The Smoking Gun," meaning locating some specific, hard evidence that connected the break-in at Democratic headquarters with highly-placed men in the President's office. In the case of the Aquino assassination, the smoking gun would be a conclusive piece of evidence or closely-knit combination of facts which was more than possibility, circumstance or speculation that made the government's version of the killing prove to be false.

There were certain items of hard data:

Fact: Before, during and immediately after the Aquino assassination, the actions of security men in and out of uniform ran contrary to human expectations – in fact, they were downright peculiar. In almost all instances the men assigned to the area looked the other way, hid out, stood disinterestedly, or (in the case of the security man at the head of the stairway) turned and walked off once it was sure the two men on the tarmac were dead. The guards assigned to escort Aquino actually ran away. Security men handled the alleged murder weapon, making fingerprinting impossible. These constituted strange and suspicious evidence, but did not prove that the supposed protection of Senator Aquino was a fraud. One would have expected that professional duty, training or just curiosity would have drawn almost all the "close-in" security to look toward or rush to the violent scene. Yet perhaps there was a rational explanation for this unusual military behavior: Strict orders to guard the periphery at all costs, stay out of the way of the men in the van, or conflicting orders. On the other hand, it may have stemmed from fear of what one might be about to witness and a desire not to get involved.

Fact: There was a concentrated and fairly effective effort to keep the media from viewing the action from the moment Aquino left the plane until the alleged assassin was definitely dead. Then the AVSECOM soldiers would be pictured in a flurry of action. Not only did bodies and hands block the television cameras, but the local media had been kept at the entrance to the jetway at Gate 8 well away from terminal windows looking out on the tarmac. However, this could be explained by some natural antagonism of security men to the media, orders to move Aquino without public surveillance, to keep the media away from the true action route, or stupidity.

Fact: Sergeant deMesa and one of the guards each said, "I'll do it" part way down the stairway, and two different men called out "Shoot" or "Shoot him" about one second before Aquino was shot. The "I'll do it" could refer to anything, but the "Shoot him" cries were harder to explain. They did not appear in the government's story and did not mesh with it.

Fact: After his death Aquino's body was first seen face down at a distance of approximately seven to nine feet from his feet to the bottom of the stairway. The alleged assassin was found on his back, at a right angle in front and to the left of Aquino.

Fact: Sergeant deMesa had felt Aquino for weapons and bullet proof vest.

Fact: Aquino was shot once in the back of the neck and the bullet exited in the chin with both entry and exit holes relatively small.

Fact: Aquino and the alleged assassin were within the same range of height, despite considerable controversy and inaccurate and changing government reports of the heights.

Fact: Despite some denials, before Aquino left Taipei the government had knowledge that he was on the China Airlines flight 811.

Fact: The alleged assassin was shot once in the back of the head, twice in the back and several times in the chest.

Fact: It was approximately 9.2 seconds from the time Aquino took the first step down the stairway until the firing of the shot that killed him.

Fact: It was about 3.5 seconds from the time Aquino was shot until the firing of the first of four shots in a volley apparently at the alleged killer.

Fact: Five men, four uniformed (deMesa, Lat, Lazaga and Moreno) and one plainclothesman (Miranda) accompanied Aquino down the stairway. At least one other plainclothesman stood outside on the platform until both Aquino and the alleged gunman were down on the tarmac, and then re-entered the jetway.

Fact: Approximately 20 seconds after Aquino was shot the doors to the AVSECOM van were only slightly ajar and several men remained inside.

Fact: Most, if not all, of the chest wounds and the elbow wound on the alleged assassin came from shots fired into him while he lay on his back on the ground.

Fact: The alleged killer had rivulets of blood running uphill, contrary to gravitational flow, on his cheeks and forehead although he was on his back.

Fact: The immediate scene around the alleged gunman was altered between the time the van pulled away and the body was ready to be transported several hours later. A holster had moved or brought in so that it was close to the body, and several unused bullets were placed next to the body either from Galman's pocket or elsewhere.

Fact: Aquino's eyeglasses were placed near the alleged assassin's body some time during the afternoon and they were unbroken.

Fact: Two of the escorts to Aquino (Lazaga and Moreno)

wore holsters, but whether they contained guns cannot be determined.

Fact: Nowhere in the pictures of the alleged killer on the ground is there any identification, badge or pass shown on his collars or shirt front.

Fact: There were security men – both in and out of uniform – deployed at various points under the plane, including behind the stairway, prior to Aquino being brought down.

Fact: No one called any warning to the guards or to Aquino prior to Aquino's being shot.

Probability: Despite Munoz's belated conversion to a bouncing bullet theory, the chances were that the trajectory of the fatal bullet was downward. It was theoretically possible, however, that a bullet could enter upward and then tumble. The original autopsy reported a forward and downward course. Munoz's insistence on the downward trajectory as a richochet off bone must remain a theory and his elimination of the more likely possibility of a downward aim was an unscientific approach.

Probability: The alleged killer made no effort to escape, whether he was the shooter of Aquino or not.

Probability: The .357 Smith and Wesson revolver was an unlikely candidate to be the death weapon because of the relatively small exit wound in the chin. However, this was not a one hundred percent hypothesis, because if the bullet lost considerable mass within the head it was possible that the exit would not have blown off much of Aquino's face. There are three fragments which did not add up to enough to reduce the exit damage. Despite Olivas' claim, the ballistics report did not determine the .357 was the murder weapon.

Probability: The alleged gunman was never behind Aquino, but appeared in front of him just as he was shot or a split second thereafter. It appeared that he was shot 3.5 seconds after Aquino while standing up.

Probability: There were many more eyewitnesses to the actual event – including several plainclothes agents caught by the cameras shortly afterward – who had never been identified or come forward.

Probability: That if the trajectory were downward or even initially level Aquino had to have been shot by someone on an elevated location and the only elevated site was the stairway from the jetway.

Laid out in the preceding fashion there seemed to be a strong circumstantial case for rebuttal and destruction of the government's version of the assassination. Yet, this refutation was still only circumstantial since the key time period was still cloaked in mystery.

On the other hand, the government had six "eyewitness" participants who backed up the official narrative. Somehow the killer sneaked up on Aquino between the bottom of the stairs and the van door; he fired; he spun away – bumped by deMesa – and was either shot by one or more AVSECOM soldiers as he was falling or after he fell; the unarmed escorts scattered, but deMesa pulled himself together and ran over and picked up the murder gun which had fallen from the killer's hand. The autopsy physician now contended the trajectory of Aquino's fatal bullet had been caused by its striking bone.

Suspicion, probability and possibility would not make it.

If there was to be a smoking gun – other than an outright confession – it had to lie somewhere during the period when the television cameras had lost sight of Aquino as he took his first step down the stairway and the first photos of the two men dead on the tarmac. This time span was a total of less than 30 seconds. Whether the events had been more or less as the government claimed or otherwise, a lot had happened in that half minute.

The so-called smoking gun did exist.

It was to be found in three items of hard evidence which fitted together to form the proof that the government's version was a lie.

The first essential piece was found in the most unlikely place: The admittedly faulty and partially fictional re-enactment of the crime which had been prepared under the direction of General Olivas.

In the government's production shown on Manila television, the actor playing Aquino came down the actual staircase in the grip of two AVSECOM men. One was at each elbow. The three were jammed together with Aquino slightly in front. They were moving down the stairs as fast as possible. Their movement was swift, almost ludicrously so — like an old silent movie. They could not have descended faster without the risk of falling.

The authors' stopwatch was started with the first step on the top platform and was punched "stop" as the first foot of the man portraying Aquino touched the ground: 9.5 seconds. Again the videotape was run through the Betamax. Again the stopwatch stopped at 9.5 seconds.

Where was Aquino when he was shot? Now the world would know. According to both the TBS and ABC videotape sound tracks, the first fatal gunshot came 9.2 seconds after Aquino took his first step onto the platform at the head of the stairs.

The government's re-enactment proved conclusively that even at near breakneck speed it took over nine seconds to reach the ground, Senator Aquino could not have taken more than one step onto the tarmac when he was shot.

There was no way around this simple physical fact. During the time that the eyes of the cameras were blinded, Aquino and his escorts could only have made it to the bottom of the stairway and no farther.

The second interlocking hard piece in the puzzle was the cry of "Pusila" ("Shoot him"), followed by another order of "Pusila" a second before the shot that killed Aquino. This order to shoot him, which came from the stairs or from someone close by, could only have been meant for the Senator. Under both versions, in back (government) or in front (Wakamiya and Ueda), Galman did not appear until after Aquino was shot.

Dropping into place to complete the picture was the position of the two bodies. Since Aquino was shot at the bottom of the stairs and the order to shoot him came while he was still on the stairway, Galman could not have been anywhere but in front of Aquino. His final resting place on the tarmac with his feet close to Aquino's head (as if he had fallen backward while facing him) was totally consistent and required no contortions. Galman did not flee for several reasons, including the fact that he was not the assassin.

Even taken separately, each piece of evidence pulled the underpinning from the governmental story of the crime. Locked together they shattered the involved story of the assassin running from under the stairway and catching up several steps later. The re-enactment timed the shooting some four seconds too late. No longer could the assassin be pictured as stumbling and falling for some three and one-half seconds, since he could not have fired the fatal shot.

The man in blue jeans "standing at a loss" "in front of Aquino" described by the contained Ueda and the flamboyant Wakamiya became plausible when the tale of his shooting Aquino from behind dissolved.

The "bouncing bullet" of Dr. Munoz suddenly straightened out as he had originally reported. So the fatal shot had to have come from the only elevated position available: Somewhere on the stairway.

There can be no doubt Aquino had to have been shot no later than the instant he touched ground. All occurrences had to be in tune with the salient, immutable fact that it took more than nine seconds to descend the 19-step staircase. And the irony was that the Metrocom Chief General Olivas – having the stairway available to conduct the re-enactment – provided the proof that the government's version was a gross fabrication.

It had been assumed by the authors – and everyone else who tried to examine the facts – that Aquino had fallen forward exactly where he was shot. Since he probably could not have made the eight or nine feet to where his feet were found, it became obvious that his escorts heaved his dying body forward immediately after the death blow.

This would explain Wakamiya's description of his falling "like a log" instead of crumbling as the nerve line from brain to body ceased to function. It would also explain the streak of blood underneath his body to the main pool where his head came to rest. But most of all that brutal heave would be the cause of the severe abrasions around the eyes reported in the official autopsy. Senator Aquino's limp form was thrown forward on his face – his shatter-proof eyeglasses knocked off by the force of the concussion from the bullet passing through his head.

His immediate escorts would have had to get out of sight since their shirts would be splattered with blood – not from the shot, but from moving the bleeding body.

The United States had its Watergate to hide official involvement in a cheap burglary and wire tap. The Philippines now had its "Manilagate" to cover up a calculated political murder.

The realization that the government's version of the killing of Ninoy Aquino was a fabrication prompted a re-assessment of the investigation. No longer was the authors' prime concern digging through the mass of material to sort out the facts from speculation, or evidence from opinion. It was to track down a conspiracy.

The assassination had to be a conspiracy, involving a broad number of both active and passive participants. Who was involved? How was the conspiracy devised? Did it have a motive more basic than the death of one man?

There was also the eerie realization that much of what the various governmental spokesmen and defenders had been saying – the reports they were giving and their supposed investigations – were all a tangle of lies and half-truths to cover-up the crime.

How could the authors determine what was real and what was false in the face of the coordinated effort to shield the truth?

We would start with the most obvious false lead: The lone assassin.

CHAPTER 13

Galman: Villain or Victim

So where did that leave the bloating body of the man in blue jeans riddled full of .45 and armalite bullets?

For nine days there were regular announcements by General Olivas that the search for the killer's identity was continuing. The dead man's picture was published. It was announced that he had a ring with an "R" and underpants embroidered with "Rolly." Each bulletin on him reinforced his role as the established assassin and kept the attention of the public on the police work in tracking down his name.

Finally, on the ninth day after the killings, it was formally announced that the killer was Rolando Galman y Dawang, a 33-year-old "notorious gun-for-hire" (to quote Olivas) and that identification had been achieved by fingerprint comparisons. Actually, as President Marcos would later mention with some bewilderment, Olivas knew his identity for two days before it was announced in a report by Olivas to his commander, General Fabian Ver.

According to extensive police records, Galman had been a member of a smalltown gang of toughs, and had been arrested on suspicion of murder, possession of firearms, car-napping and a botched gas station hold-up in which he got slashed in the leg with a bolo for his efforts. He had reached the peak of his career as part of a gang caught for armed robbery of 34,000 pesos.

His bully boys were suspected of murders, including the death of an informer who was shot the day he was released.

In his last brush with the law, for reasons that were not clear, Galman was arrested under a Presidential Commitment Order personally signed by President Marcos. Such orders were reserved for political detainees. Held in a military facility, Galman was eventually bailed out in November, 1982, when two Manila businessmen reportedly put up bail of 40,000 pesos.

Back in his home town he had a 63-year-old mother, who would later claim he was only a "simple farmer" although she admitted she had not seen him for four years. He also had a 20-year-old sister. In another town there was a common-law wife named Lina Lozano and a young son, Rey (variously reported to be one and nine years old). According to the Filipino tabloid, *Tempo*, the neighbors reported that Rolando was going to marry Lina in the Catholic Church in San Miguel, Bulacan, on August 26 (five days after his death) with a roast pig and the works.

Reporters for *Asiaweek*, the English-language magazine published in Hong Kong, and Reuters, claimed Galman also had a girlfriend, Anna "Baby" Oliva (variously reported to be named Ana and Alma), an entertainer at the Del Monte supper club in Manila. According to the reporters who interviewed "Baby", she spent the last three nights of Galman's life with him at an airport motel. More significantly, at all times five armed men with close cropped hair were with them or guarding the door.

Asiaweek also reported that "Baby" found Galman depressed and when she asked him why, he replied in Tagalog: "This is a heavy mission. It's beyond you," but added: "Monday, we'll go shopping."

All of these stories must be approached warily, since they are borderline hearsay. However, *Tempo* and other news sources reported that on August 27, three days *before* Galman was identified as the alleged assassin, his mother Saturnina Dawang and sister, Marilyn, were picked up by the Air Force. These women were kept incommunicado. *Tempo* also said that the would-be wife and son had been taken by military-looking men before

Galman was identified as the dead killer, and that their where-abouts were unknown. Three months later, at Galman's funeral the son (about two years old) re-appeared but the common law wife did not. One evening in September, Miss Oliva and her sister, Catherine, were picked up by investigators and driven around in a military car for several hours and then released. The topic of the conversation was not known. The Oliva girls reportedly have not been seen since.

Despite General Olivas' contention (made the day of Galman's identification) that Galman had been hired by "subversive" groups, there was nothing in his lengthy criminal record to support that theory. His entire profile was that of a small town tough with an eye for the good life. Nevertheless, as time would tell, the government would not let that theory die.

The night of the assassination President Marcos had expressed the belief that it was impossible to stop a man who was willing to trade his own life in an assassination attempt. Obviously this was inconsistent with Galman's gun-for-hire designation.

Since the government's claim that Galman was a lone assassin striking from behind had gone up in smoke, what was the true role of the second man lying dead on the tarmac with Senator Aquino? Whatever way his role was explained to him, and under what circumstances, as he saw it, Galman intended to survive. What the men who got him to the scene told him can only be speculated. His participation had to fall into one of the following categories: 1) He was not acting out of philosophical commitment for he had none; 2) He was not acting under any personal animosity, since he had no connection with Aquino; 3) He acted for money, to return a favor, or because he was forced to.

If "Baby's" story were to be believed, Galman was apprehensive about his participation but could not avoid it. From her description the plot involved military or paramilitary men. However, he would be free to go shopping the day after the event so he was not planning to hide out.

125

Those who chose Galman knew that there was no exit for him other than death. But Galman was not aware of that. The people who involved Galman also recognized that his unsavory past would make him a likely suspect – especially if he could not talk.

Presuming that Galman was street smart, he would not believe that he could assassinate a prominent man in broad daylight surrounded by guards and witnesses and survive. There seem to be only three possibilities of what he was told to seduce him into participating: 1) That he would be an assassin but someone else would be immediately blamed; 2) He was to be given a lesser role such as delivering or getting rid of a murder weapon, or being a false witness; or 3) He was to be an assassin at some other place than the airport and would be spirited away.

Whatever he was told, it was a lie.

Whatever way he got to the tarmac beside China Airlines Flight 811, it was not by infiltrating security, but he was brought there. Look around the scene photographed by Wakamiya (PIC–1) as the plane halted. Somewhere out there was Rolando Galman.

Richard Vokey, reporting from Manila in the September 26 issue of *Newsweek*, wrote:

> Military sources told *Newsweek* that the alleged assassin had a close relationship with Col. Arturo Custodio (apparently no close relative of General Luther Custodio, the former chief of AVSECOM), an Air Force officer attached to the headquarters of General Ver. The colonel grew up in the same town as Galman, and, according to *Newsweek*'s sources, employed him to do occasional light work until less than a week before the Aquino killing. Some of Custodio's Air Force colleagues thought it unusual that the colonel would have hired a notorious gunman like Galman as a retainer. Custodio himself is regarded with some trepidation; by reputation he is a tough man who "get things done."

UPI's Max Vanzi reportedly had a line on the same story, but returned to the United States before he could follow it up.

This had all the earmarks of just an unverified rumor, until November 9, when Colonel Custodio came before the newly-constituted investigation commission. The colonel denied having hired Galman, but admitted he had met him about four years previously at a party and found out they had been neighbors in the colonel's home town.

Custodio also stated that he had helped Galman's attorney arrange to see Galman when he had been arrested in 1982 and was being held in military prison. After Galman got out on bail he had visited the colonel's home several times, but the colonel said he did not think this improper because the young man had never been sentenced for any crime.

Colonel Custodio went on to describe a drinking spree with Galman at the colonel's home in July. Custodio quoted Galman as telling him at that time: "I have something to follow up. My group instructed me." He described Galman as despondent over something "he could not run away from, although he wanted to run away."

Despite the fact that he was a high-ranking Air Force security officer attached to the general staff, Colonel Custodio claimed he did not try to find out what Galman was about. He also said he did not recognize Galman's picture in the paper until ten days after his death.

All this was hard to believe. That Galman unburdened himself to this military man about an assassination plot, even by implication, strained credulity. That the colonel would not try to find out what the "group" was and what deed it had instructed Galman to perform, would be a remarkable admission of incompetence.

What is far more believable is that like a good security man Colonel Custodio had helped a charming rogue get out of military prison by arranging for his lawyer to get bail, and then befriended him for strong-arm activities or as a patsy in some security operation. Who better but a tough from the home town who owes his freedom to you? A little money, some good times, a willing girl from a local club...and then just one little job.

But enough of Galman in life. He will tell us more in death.

Imelda Marcos

President Ferdinand E. Marcos

Major General Prospero Olivas, Chief of Metrocom, head of military investigation of death of Aquino

General Fabian C. Ver, Chief of Staff of the Armed Forces.

The escort group appears before Fernando Commission: (l. to r.) Constabularyman 1st Class Rogelio Moreno, Constabularyman 1st Class Mario Lazaga, Sgt. Arnulfo deMesa, Sgt. Claro Lat, and 2nd Lt. Jesus Castro; general counsel Rustico Nazareno at right foreground.

Rosendo Cawigan, supposed undercover man

Corazon Agrava, chairperson of restructured commission

Andres R. Narvasa, counsel for new commission

Brigadier General Luther Custodio, chief of AVSECOM

Dr. Bienvenido Munoz demonstrates with skull

Luis Tabuena, manager, Manila International Airport.

130

CHAPTER 14

If At First...

A month after Aquino's death, on September 20, General Olivas presented to Chief Justice Fernando, still hanging on as chairman of the investigation commission, the "Second Status Report on the Investigation of the Killing of Ex-Senator Benigno S. Aquino, Jr."

It had been a tough month for the Metrocom chief. While thousands of young people ran through the streets wearing yellow T-shirts reading "Who Killed Ninoy Aquino?", the foreign press was probing about and asking some provocative questions. Little gatherings around Manila sat before Betamaxes watching videotapes of the Japanese news specials, while in Manila's financial district of Makati corporate presidents and secretaries mingled in the streets demanding governmental reforms and Marcos' resignation.

On the other hand, General Olivas now knew what questions had been raised about what he had been telling the public. A detailed, authoritative report of his investigation might help silence the doubters and answer many of the more persistent questions.

Olivas' so-called second report opened with a detailed discussion of the orders and responsibilities of the Philippine Constabulary, the armed forces and AVSECOM. Then Olivas repeated the story that AVSECOM had "checked" nine incoming airliners prior to the arrival of China Airlines Flight No. 811, because there were "uncertainties" and "conflicting reports" as to which aircraft would be carrying Senator Aquino.

Why he persisted in that falsehood cannot be fully understood, except once told he might have felt that lie could not be recanted. (Eventually it was.) None of the other airliners was boarded by Philippine government officials, and sometime between Thursday and Saturday morning the Philippine government knew Aquino was coming from Taipei.

Olivas reported that five men boarded the plane – 2nd Lt. Jesus Castro, Lat, deMesa, Lazaga and Moreno. He described their movements in meeting Aquino pretty much as the television cameras had portrayed. For the first time it was admitted that an undercover agent accompanied the four uniformed men in escorting Aquino down the stairway. The plainclothesman shown following Aquino out the door (TV–17) was identified as T. Sgt. Filomeno Miranda. According to the second report, Lat handed Aquino's overnight bag to Miranda. As it would eventually turn out, Miranda was the man in the white shirt seen running to the car under the terminal after the shooting was over (TV–27).

The second report also revealed that Lt. Castro – watching the operation – reported by radio to AVSECOM headquarters that Aquino was aboard. Apparently, AVSECOM commander General Custodio was on the other end, because the report stated that "Custodio ordered that Ex-Senator Aquino be escorted through the stairway and loaded in the AVSECOM van at the tarmac." This seemed odd since the original plan, according to Olivas, had been to do just that. Therefore, the newly-stated order was superfluous.

A team of seven undercover agents from AVSECOM had been placed "to provide security coverage in tunnel 8." This group was under the command of Capt. Romeo Bautista, who sent two of his men to "check a group of people gathered at bay 7." Gathered at Gate 8 were the local television crew, cameramen and local reporters, unaware that Aquino was not going to be brought along that jetway. Bautista's men could maintain order at the gate and, not incidentally, keep reporters and other observers away from the windows between Gates 7 and 8.

Instead of the three men shown in the re-enactment, the report now accounted for five men accompanying Aquino down the stairway. Sgt. deMesa was holding Aquino on the left, and T. Sgt. Lat held him on the right. Constabularyman Moreno "was following behind." Then came Constabularyman T. Sgt. Miranda, dressed in a polo barong and carrying Aquino's bag. He was followed by Lazaga who was carrying some "other" hand luggage of Aquino.

The actual shooting was described as follows:

> As Ex-Senator Aquino was being led to the AVSECOM van, suddenly a man in light blue shirt darted towards him and shot him from behind. When C1C (Constabularyman First Class) Lazaga was about three (3) rungs on the stairway from the ground, he noticed a man with a blue shirt and denim pants dart toward the back of Sgt. deMesa, and suddenly fired a gun at the back of the head of Ex-Senator Aquino. Upon hearing the gunfire, he immediately ran for cover and heard successive shots. Sgt. Arnulfo deMesa felt an object touch his shoulder and almost simultaneously a shot rang out. He warded off the object that touched his shoulder, which turned out to be the gunman, who was thrown off balance, and was shot successively by his companions from the SWAT van.

This portion of the report was noteworthy for its lack of details as to time, exactly how Galman wound up on his back, and why he made no effort to get away.

Olivas described in military terms the deployment of four SWAT teams of AVSECOM's 805th Special Operations Squadron, under Capt. Felipe Valerio, in a mix of Greek letters and American military code names: ALFA, BRAVO, CHARLIE and DELTA. DELTA "secured" the front section of the plane. These appear to have been the men hunkered down in TV–26. BRAVO and CHARLIE "secured" the rear section. Meanwhile

ALFA stayed in the van to await Aquino. It was as if by invoking this military terminology Olivas proved something was done. What "secured" meant in this context was not explained. Why ALFA stayed out of sight in the van until all the damage was done was not explained.

Six of the participants, according to the report, saw the shooting:

Constabularyman Lazaga, fifth in line on the stairway, "while three rungs up, watched Galman dart toward the back of Sgt. deMesa, and suddenly fired a gun towards the back of the head of Ex-Senator Aquino." Lazaga said nothing, he shouted no warning, he took no action except to run and hide somewhere after the first shot. He just let his compatriot deMesa take his chances while the gunman ran up behind him, and then he watched in stunned silence as Galman shot their charge, Senator Aquino.

But the report showed he did do something: "Upon hearing the gunfire, he immediately ran for cover and heard successive shots." To run for cover he had to head down the stairs toward the killer, and then go somewhere.

Sgt. deMesa attempted to explain how Galman wound up on his back in front of Aquino's body. The sergeant said he knocked the killer off balance as he heard the shot. As per his own story, deMesa stood there while Galman was shot and "then ran, picked up the gun of the fallen gunman, a Caliber .357 Revolver, and sought cover behind the van." This, of course, was a sharp discrepancy from the re-enactment, in which deMesa ran off to the left, dropped to the tarmac, and then arose without coming near the dead assassin.

The report said nothing about deMesa's grip on Aquino's arm when his prisoner was shot, nor about any other details. The sergeant's conduct defies normal expectations. If he had thought there was a chance the killer was still able to use the revolver he would have either gotten out of the way or would have kicked it away rather than picking it up. However, he was stuck with Olivas' explanation made the date of the assassination.

Sgt. Romeo Fernandez, the next "eyewitness," was a member of one of the SWAT teams under the plane, and identified as a "ramp guard" in the second Olivas report. Sgt. Fernandez "noticed the gunman. . .dash toward the back of a man dressed in white (Ex-Senator Aquino). The man quickly pulled out a gun and then Sgt. Fernandez heard a gunshot. He saw the man in white fall, face down. He also witnessed SWAT personnel fire at the assailant." This version is so void of detail, Fernandez could have gotten it from the newspapers. Where was he? How was the assailant killed? Where did the SWAT personnel come from?

Captain Llewelyn Kavinta, the leader of Delta Team, "recalled that while he was in his pre-designated position in front of the aircraft, he heard a shot, prompting him to look back and he saw a man holding a gun behind Ex-Senator Aquino and his escorts. The gunman was shot by members of the SWAT team." If Captain Kavinta heard the shot and then saw Galman standing behind Aquino, he not only reversed the chronology but he was at odds with deMesa's story.

Master Sergeant Pablo Martinez, a deployed AVSECOM man and another "eyewitness" named in the report "recounted that he saw a man in blue shirt behind Ex-Senator Aquino. At the same time he heard a gunshot. He sought cover immediately behind a tug."

Sgt. Rolando de Guzman claimed to have been cut from sterner stuff. In the report "Guzman stated that when Ex-Senator Aquino was nearing the van with his escorts, he saw a man suddenly appear from behind the former Senator with a gun and then fired. He in turn fired at the gunman." His story was so sparse as to be nearly meaningless. As it would turn out, de Guzman would get a later chance to amplify on his role in the event.

In regard to other shots fired at Galman, the report stated that he was shot by several men who had been waiting in the van: A1C (Airman First Class) Cordova Estelo, with a .45 pistol, T. Sgt. Rodolfo Desolong with his .45, S. Sgt. Ernesto Mateo with his M16, and S. Sgt. Pedrito Torio, a ramp guard, fired "a warning shot" with his Super .38 pistol. When, in what order, to what effect, how many times? Simple questions with no answers.

Apparently Sergeant Lat at Aquino's right side, as well as Sergeant Miranda and Constabularyman Moreno, both following on the staircase, saw and heard nothing, for they were not listed among the eyewitnesses. Neither was the blasé security man on the platform who was seen and photographed watching the later stages of the event by the ABC camera.

The blocking and eventual locking of the door to the stairway was explained. Lieutenant Castro could not follow the escort group because he was busy controlling "unruly passengers" who tried to force their way through the door leading to the bridge stairway. Then he heard gunfire. The crowd surged toward the door to the stairway, compelling him to close the door with the assistance of S. Sgt. Pelias, S. Sgt. delaCruz, S. Sgt. Danao, and Airman Febrero.

Olivas' report also reiterated that the "escorts who were near him (Aquino) at the time of the shooting were unarmed."

As part of the second report Olivas released the NBI ballistics report which proved that both the magnum's distorted shell supposedly found on the tarmac and the particles found in Aquino's head were lead.

The report also noted that deMesa had turned the magnum revolver over to Master Sergeant Pablo Martinez, presumably after Martinez came out from behind the "tug."

General Olivas also reported that he personally took pictures of the crime scene on the afternoon of August 21. "While taking pictures, he noticed what appeared to be a MIA Temporary Pass, clipped to the left collar of the gunman's shirt." The pass was in the name of a Sergeant Dominador Aguayo of the Philippine Air Force, who, it turned out, had reported it lost in January, 1982. The report speculated that this was the means by which Galman had infiltrated security.

The problem with this wonderful find is that the pass did not show up in any of the pictures taken immediately after Galman's death and had not been noticed by the reporters who earlier had been shown the body.

136

Finally, General Olivas detailed a change of plans on the handling of Aquino as ordered by General Fabian C. Ver. But that was just another chapter in the matter of the various contingent plans and became a story in itself.

Somehow Mark Fineman, reporter for the Knight News Service, got a long look at more than 100 pages of background documents which formed the basis for the report. In a story in the October 31 edition of *The Philadelphia Inquirer*, Fineman was able to add a considerable amount of detail contained in the supposed interviews.

Escort Moreno "suddenly heard a gunshot... prompting him to run to the building post about 10 meters (11 yards) away to seek cover."

Sgt. Torio, who fired the "warning shot" after both men were dead, was under the left wing of the plane "to see to it that no unauthorized person got near..." Then how did he miss seeing Galman who supposedly emerged from that direction?

Airman Joseph Opilas was a ramp guard standing at the bottom of the stairway with his M16, but he was facing away to see that "no one approached the airplane. At that time a shot rang out," and he "glanced back and saw the man in white fall."

DeGuzman, who told the skeletal story of shooting at the assailant, had his story fleshed out in the background interview report: "a man suddenly appeared from the rear holding a gun pointed at (Aquino) and fired." He instantly drew his .45-caliber revolver "but was unable to fire immediately at the gunman because he might hit Sgt. deMesa." Then he was "able to fire at the gunman and used up all my bullets," from his .45.

Sergeant DeGuzman apparently did not know that the sound tracks revealed only four shots in the first volley and most likely two of those came from different guns since they were virtually simultaneous. Nor did his story explain a 3.5 second hesitation when deMesa either ran away (re-enactment) or stood still while Galman spun clear (report statement).

According to these interviews Sergeant Ernesto Mateo pumped 9 shots from his M16 into Galman's corpse. Airman Cordova Estolo, who followed Mateo (the photos show the man with the M16 firing last) shot his .45 three times and Sgt. Rudolfo Desolong, group leader of Alfa, also took three shots from his .45 handgun. To this point government reports state that 21 shots had been fired at Galman.

There was no explanation of how so many must have missed, of the shot behind the ear or the two in the back (although deGuzman might have hit the twisting Galman in the back – unless Galman was actually standing in front of Aquino).

Sgt. Reuben Aquino (no relation), probably the man with his cap on backwards who appeared to be aiming at the ground, missed out on the heroics, but his shots are not in the tally of 21. He fired his M16 once but hit the bumper of the van before his gun jammed.

Where was Galman when DeGuzman shot him? In what direction was he facing? The report remained silent on those key points.

Reporter Fineman noted that there were interviews of 80 military men and 20 civilians in the area, but there were no additional witnesses found.

As "the" major document in the cover-up the second Olivas report was a bust. An attempt to mesh known facts such as placement of the bodies, known bullet wounds, and number and sequence of shots with the fiction of the lone assassin running from under the plane – past a mass of trained army men – was an impossible task.

CHAPTER 15

Commission and Omission

Although President Marcos had promised that the powers of the government would be used to bring those responsible for the Aquino assassination to a "speedy" justice, the commission to investigate the assassination was scarcely the vehicle for it. In the first place, its composition guaranteed that it would not be much more than window dressing to confirm the findings of the military investigation being conducted by General Olivas.

Named as chairman of the commission was Enrique Fernando, Chief Justice of the Philippine Supreme Court. The other appointed members were former justices, 68 to 80 years of age. All of them had been political allies and appointees of the President. In response to an immediate complaint by leaders of the opposition, Marcos made an attempt to get Jaime Cardinal Sin to serve on the commission. The leader of the Philippine Catholic Church, Cardinal Sin had often voiced criticism of the more totalitarian aspects of the Marcos regime, had complained about the arrest of active priests, and had called for national reconciliation and electoral and economic reforms. Sin declined the appointment.

The commission plodded through the choice of several legal counsel and announced it was going to call as witnesses the Generals – Olivas and Custodio – who had been in charge of security on the fateful day. It became the repository for reports such as the autopsies, but by the first week in September it had not conducted any independent investigation.

The commission's first hearing in early September heard Dr. Munoz expound on his theory of the deflected bullet turning downward when it struck bone. Although assistant counsel Seno made an attempt to ask follow-up questions, he was limited to direct examination. Over the protests of opposition attorneys no cross-examination was allowed even by prominent apolitical attorneys.

Immediately after that hearing, Chairman Fernando suspended the commission's activity on the ground that he had to await the results of three law suits challenging the commission's legality. Among the arguments against the commission was that by putting the Chief Justice in charge, there was a violation of separation of powers – judicial and executive. The underlying complaint was that the commission was neither independent nor impartial. Marcos retorted that the opposition wanted to halt the commission's work because it did not want the facts. Although its staff continued to receive reports, in effect the commission did very little.

Eventually, on October 1, Chairman Fernando resigned. President Marcos immediately named as his successor a member of his cabinet, Minister of State for Foreign Affairs, Arturo Tolentino. Minister Tolentino was out of the country attending a law of sea conference and would not return until October 5. Another hearing was scheduled for October 10.

Instead of holding a hearing, the commission announced that Tolentino had decided to reject the appointment as Chairman. The other members resigned en masse with a written statement that "We cannot work in an atmosphere of disbelief." Tolentino had been more blunt, stating it was a "waste of time and money."

Out with the commission went its staff. In a fit of either righteous indignation or pique, assistant counsel Seno – who had hesitated to dig into Munoz' statement – announced the results of paraffin tests conducted by the NBI on the 14 close-in AV-

SECOM men: Sergeant deMesa and Constable Moreno were both positive for nitrates on their hands. While only four specks had been found on Moreno's hands, deMesa (who had been at Aquino's left) had 12 such specks of nitrate on his hands. Seno also mentioned that one of the five escort guards had not been tested, but did not mention which one.

While such tests are conducted to determine if one has fired a gun in the recent past, they are not conclusive. If one was close to a gun that was fired, handled a recently-fired gun, or was a heavy smoker, they might show positive. Even opposition lawyer Jose W. Diokno was quoted as saying such tests are "in no way conclusive" that the men fired guns.

What was interesting was that the test results had not been made public for more than a month after they had been submitted to the commission. Galman's positive results for nitrates had been reported promptly. If attorney Seno had not decided on his last day on the job to release the findings they might still be secret.

The conduct of the commission had been strange from the start. Its general counsel, Rustico Nazareno, had promised that a panel of responsible lawyers would be allowed to cross-examine but then changed his mind. The five military escorts (but not plainclothesman Miranda) were introduced to the commission on October 5 when their names were revealed, but there had been no questioning.

Phil Bronstein of the *San Francisco Examiner* called the opening-day hearing marked by "confusion, disbelief and mistrust." With the commission's demise in October, Mark Fineman of Knight News Service, reporting in the *Philadelphia Inquirer*, stated flatly that the commission's staff had been "lax" and cited some examples:

"More than 200 airline passengers in the area at the time of the killing have not yet been sought for questioning.

"No subpoenas have been issued for the government TV crew that was filming at the airport.

"The death of a general who might have warned Aquino of an assassination had not been investigated."

The general to whom correspondent Fineman referred was Brigadier General Baltazar Aguirre, Philippine Constabulary Intelligence Chief. Fineman reported that Aguirre who was "widely believed to be a secret information source for Aquino was killed in a freak accident September 23, when a 10-wheel truck slammed into his van on a deserted highway and pushed it into the path of a second truck."

Details of the accident reported in the Philippine newspapers were that driving from a night meeting with General Fidel Ramos, Philippine Constabulary Chief of Staff, with his wife as a passenger, Aguirre's van was side-swiped by a hit and run truck and thrown in front of a container truck coming in the opposite direction. General Aguirre and his wife both died despite the efforts of the second truck driver to rush them to the hospital. The hit and run truck was never found, and the driver of the on-coming container truck was arrested.

Having made little progress in investigating the death of Aquino, to expect the commission to look into the suspicious death of General Aguirre was probably asking the impossible. If the General had been the source of the warning telephone calls to Aquino in Taipei, he was in a position to expose the cover-up. And if he were Aquino's source his death was a happy convenience to the conspirators.

Not to have interviewed Maharlika Broadcasting television personnel at the airport was inexcusable for such an investigative commission. Airport manager Luis Tabuena had told Reporter Fineman that a month before the assassination jurisdiction over the television and the automatic surveillance cameras had been turned over to AVSECOM. When the persistent correspondent had asked commission counsel Nazareno if he had interviewed Tabuena about the matter Nazareno replied: "It must have slipped my mind. I guess I'll have to get back to him on that."

At a meeting with the Mindanao (the most southerly Philippine island) press corps in early October, Minister of Information Gregorio Cendaña was asked if it were true that the government videotape had stopped just before Aquino emerged from the plane. Cendaña answered that indeed there was a gap, because the shooting startled the cameraman who "ran for cover."

The obvious faulty logic in Cendaña's explanation made the episode of the missing footage (reminiscent of President Nixon's secretary's tape missing 18 minutes of dictation) highly suspect. Since the shooting of the film began with the killing of Aquino, at least that moment should have been recorded. The image of the cameraman safe inside the terminal building abandoning his task at the sound of what must have been a mere "pop" to his ears was hard to picture. Somehow, the cowardly cameraman picked up his courage to return to his post after the dust had settled. The Maharlika videotape came back on once the van with Ninoy's body aboard had pulled away.

A few days after the investigating commission resigned, President Marcos signed Presidential Decree No. 1886, which was intended to replace the commission with a restructured body of seven. Before it would begin its work there would be a round of solicitation of recommendations of names and restaffing. In short, if the name of the cover-up game was delay, the Fernando Commission had served its purpose.

It must have been frustrating to the conspirators – whoever they were – that the embarrassing questions would not go away. The official scenario was being challenged harder than ever.

Every official-sounding report and every explanation raised more doubts. The cover-up of Manilagate was becoming a bit frayed around the edges.

CHAPTER 16

The Great Undercover Agent

Just as Justice Fernando was bowing out as commission chairman, a new actor was ushered onto the stage. Under a headline "Reds Plotted Aquino Slay, Says Agent," the *Philippines Sunday Express*, a pro-government newspaper, of October 2 carried a government press release about one Rosendo Cawigan, age 44.

Cawigan, a one-time driver and bodyguard for Senator Aquino (he says for 16 years, the Aquino family says for three), had gained fame during the military trial of the Senator by testifying against him. Then he had alleged that the Senator's home in Quezon City was a refuge for Communist guerillas who needed medical treatment. Cawigan had also testified that Aquino appeared to have advance knowledge of the Plaza Miranda bombing of a Liberal rally on August 21, 1971, and stayed away. In reality Ninoy was at a party for Assemblyman Laurel's daughter and was scheduled to be the wind-up speaker at the rally.

The story as the government told it was that since his days as a witness against Aquino, Cawigan had become an undercover agent for the government among the Communists. He claimed to have become a confidante of one Rodolfo Salas, "alias Commander Bilog," reputedly chairman of the Philippines Communist Party central committee.

Cawigan said that Bilog had asked him in May if he would be willing to assassinate Aquino, and left Cawigan to think about

145

it. According to the alleged undercover agent, he immediately informed the government of the impending plot.

He claimed that in June he had met with Bilog again and had been told that the Communists had found another gunman. Apparently the Communist leader had no hesitancy about telling Cawigan his name: Rolando Galman, better known, according to Cawigan, to the communist New People's Army as Commander Bert Ramos.

Apparently disappointed that Galman had been chosen, the press release continued, Cawigan went to Manila International Airport armed with a .45 caliber pistol on the day Aquino was to arrive. His intent was to kill Aquino if the plot failed. He said that his motive was that he had been told that Aquino would kill him for his testimony at the military trial. He got through security, he said, by using a National Bureau of Investigation identification given to him by Aquino while he was his bodyguard 11 years earlier.

The *Express* story – as did others – stated that Cawigan's report in May "became the basis for the government's warning to Aquino that there were confirmed intelligence reports about a plot to kill him upon his return from the United States."

The story was obviously to support the claim that Imelda Marcos' warning in May had some substance. Upon analysis, on almost every rational ground, it fell apart.

Cawigan was well-known for his testimony against his former employer. His use as an undercover agent among the communists (particularly since he had accused Aquino of consorting with the communists) would have been zero. If the New People's Army had been hatching a plot in May to kill Aquino, the last person the communists would have told was this man.

The most obvious fallacy was that if Cawigan knew the name of the intended killer – Rolando Galman – the government could have identified the killer in minutes and not nine days since he would have been at the head of the suspect list.

The picture of Cawigan stalking the airport – swarming with

security men – armed with a .45 and using an 11-year-old government ID strains credulity.

It was a strange sidelight to the history of the Aquino assassination. By the time Cawigan's story was released it had appeared that the government had abandoned the announced theory that the assassin was a communist himself – now that the alleged killer was Galman, a man with a "notorious criminal record." There was nothing in Galman's history that fit the pattern of ideological commitment.

Now came Cawigan – working, according to the press, as a government grain investigator – placing himself in the bosom of the communist leadership and naming Galman as "Commander Bert Ramos."

If Cawigan's tale was as fictional as it appeared, then the government's contention that Imelda's warning to Aquino in May was based on his report is obviously false. Yet the fact that the government went ahead with releasing the story as fact, showed that someone in the government thought that the story was worth floating.

That someone was President Ferdinand Marcos. On the ABC news program "Nightline," on September 22 ten days earlier, Marcos had told Ted Koppel that the government had planted an agent within the communist party who was the man who first alerted the intelligence community about the plot to assassinate Aquino. The only impediment to presenting this agent's story, Marcos said, were the cases filed against the investigating commission under Justice Fernando.

CHAPTER 17

The Fourth Contingency

The code name for the plan of AVSECOM and the military to manage the arrival of Senator Aquino on August 21 was "Operation Balikbayan", which in Tagalog means "people who return from abroad." The exact details of that plan, and even its objectives, were a matter of some conflict and possible confusion among General Olivas (Metrocom Chief from the Philippine Constabulary), General Custodio (Airport Security Chief), General Ver (Chief of the Armed Forces), 2d. Lt. Jesus Castro (Custodio's staff aide, who was put in charge of the escort party), airport manager Luis Tabuena, and President Marcos.

Early in the week before the slaying of Aquino, General Ver had announced that if Aquino arrived in the Philippines, his travel papers would be checked on the plane, and he would be sent back out by way of the very plane on which he had arrived. Publicly that announcement was not repudiated before Aquino's death.

According to the second report by Olivas to the Fernando commission, in the plan devised by Metrocom at the request of the Chief of Staff Armed Forces/Director General, National Intelligence and Security Authority (General Ver) the "Balikbayan" had been changed to bring Aquino to AVSECOM headquarters near the airport where General Custodio would check Aquino's papers, and, if they were not in order, return him to the airplane. This change had been made in a telephone

149

conversation between Olivas and Custodio on Saturday morning, according to the Olivas reports. Under this contingency plan, if Aquino were found to be properly documented he would be turned over to Major General Josephus Q. Ramas at Fort Bonifacio for imprisonment. This, of course, was impossible, since the government had refused to issue him new travel documents and Imelda Marcos had his passport.

Deputy AVSECOM commander Colonel Romeo Ochoco received the revised plan in writing on Saturday afternoon.

However, according to Olivas, General Ver called Custodio on Sunday morning, the day of Aquino's arrival, and changed the plan to a third contingency. Under Ver's plan Aquino would be arrested on the plane and brought by AVSECOM to Fort Bonifacio for incarceration.

Apparently no one bothered to inform General Olivas – if the second report is to be believed – because he told the Philippine press four days after the assassination that the plan had been to transport Aquino to AVSECOM headquarters and check his papers and, if they were not in order, to take him back to the plane. No correction or contradiction to that statement was made at the time.

Since Ver's final change was reportedly by telephone to Custodio there was no written record of that third contingency.

However, Custodio said in a brief deposition dated the day after the killing and given to Colonel Hermogenes Peralta, Jr. (the same Peralta who staged the government's re-creation of the shooting for television):

"My principal task was to secure and protect the person of Senator Benigno Aquino Jr. with specific instruction to arrest him and escort him to his former detention cell at Fort Bonifacio."

Reading the deposition raises a strong suspicion that it was actually prepared or re-written long after its date. Some of the questions were posed to provide a response to the insinuations of wrong doing by the military that had been voiced by the opposition and the foreign media. For example, the impression had been given by General Olivas that all Asian flights had been

150

checked in the same manner as China Airlines Flight 811 had been. Olivas stated this again in testimony to the Fernando Commission in September. It had been repeatedly reported by those at the airport and some foreign correspondents on the scene that all other planes from Asia were not checked. However, Custodio was asked about this (supposedly the day after the shooting when the issue had not been raised publicly) and his response was that only the exit tunnels were checked on the other planes. He went on to say that only Flight 811 was boarded, "because there were strong indications which we gathered a few minutes before the arrival of China Airlines Flight 811 that Ex-Senator Aquino was maybe on board. So I directed Lt. Castro to board said aircraft."

General Custodio did not elaborate on what the "strong indications which we gathered a few minutes before" were and how they were communicated to him. He also said that the AVSECOM van was present at all nine flights originating in Asia, but the testimony of many people at the airport indicate that this was not true. As would come out shortly, Gate 8 was receiving special security treatment for at least two days before Aquino's arrival and throughout that day.

In this same self-serving document Custodio was asked "Why did you authorize the use of the service stairs and not the usual route, that is, through the bridge [jetway]?"

Answer: "Due to the numerous intelligence reports that we received plus the condition then prevailing in and outside the terminal, I decided to authorize the use of the shortest way which I believed was the safest way, this is through the bridge stairs to the SWAT van."

The safest method, if Fort Bonifacio was the destination (or under any plan), was to order the China Airlines flight to pull up out on the runway away from the terminal and have the authorities pick up Aquino there.

The questions asked by Lt. Col. Berlin A. Castillo in the deposition are only 26 in number, and except for the few quoted above, touched in no way on how the assassination was accomplished.

Despite the fact that special medical facilities had been arranged at the airport in case of violence, Custodio said that upon being told by walkie talkie that Aquino had arrived, he radioed to Captain Valerio who was in charge of ALFA team in the van to take Aquino to Fort Bonifacio army general hospital. The time it took for those messages to be conveyed had to be less than 15 seconds.

Lt. Castro is quoted in the second Olivas report as saying that when he radioed to General Custodio the fact that Aquino was on board, he was ordered by the General to take Aquino to Fort Bonifacio. In Castro's testimony in regard to the order, no mention was made of the stairway. The reason was that it had already been decided to use said stairs. In fact at least three of the team, deMesa, Lat and Lazaga had been seen coming up the stairs before they entered the airliner.

On Wednesday, August 24, 1983, General Olivas told the media (as reported in the *Manila Evening Post*, Thursday, August 25, 1983): "If Ninoy Aquino had lived for a few more seconds, he would have been sent out of the Phillipines aboard the same jet that brought him here last Sunday..." He said Brig. Gen. Luther Custodio, head of the Aviation Security Command (AVSECOM), was standing by at the ramp to talk to Aquino.

"Custodio's orders were to ask Aquino for his travel papers, and to check if they were in order," Olivas said.

"If they were not in order, Custodio was to put Aquino back on the same plane," Olivas said...

"Olivas said this mission had been assigned to Custodio last July when Aquino announced he planned to return."

July was also the month when AVSECOM had been placed directly under the command of General Fabian Ver.

Apparently airport manager Luis Tabuena had not been brought in on any of the plans or made aware that Aquino might land on any of nine airliners arriving from Asia. Several hours earlier he had been instructed to bring the press to Gate 8.

The government version contended that Rolando Galman would have been able to follow the security people around as they rushed from one plane to another, so that was the original story. Too many people knew that was hot so. Finally, when Custodio's deposition was released many weeks after its supposed date, he admitted that while the van went around (also not true) only a routine watch was placed on passengers exiting the gates from other flights.

It was also contended by General Olivas that he had found on Galman's collar an old pass lost by a Presidential Security man issued by airport manager Tabuena in January, 1982, a year and a half before. Several dozen photographs and a large number of reporters failed to see it. But Olivas was able to trace it back to the man who had lost it through that man's commander, Colonel Rolando Abadilla, who was with General Olivas when he examined the body on the tarmac. Abadilla, according to Olivas, removed the pass from Galman's shirt and traced it back. Colonel Abadilla said that it had been reported lost in late January, 1982.

But who is Colonel Rolando Abadilla? He was not mentioned in Olivas' second report as part of the intricate chain of command assembled to protect Senator Aquino. Hard-digging Paul Quinn-Judge of the *Christian Science Monitor* described him in that newspaper's November 18 issue, stemming from an interview with two anonymous Filipino military officers:

> . . . the officers point out that Col. Rolando Abadilla, chief of the Military Intelligence and Security Group of Metrocom – the Philippine Constabulary's Metropolitan Command – was present at the airport immediately after the Aquino killing.
>
> "That man is totally ruthless," said one of the officers, "He's very dangerous."
>
> "Colonel Abadilla also has close links with another colonel, Air Force Lt. Col. Arturo Custodio, who in turn is connected to Rolando Galman, the small-time gangster alleged by the government to have shot Aquino before being himself gunned down by security forces at the airport. . .

"Abadilla – also a native of President Marcos' home province of Ilocos – has a reputation for extreme toughness. In 1968, when he was a second lieutenant, he was court-martialed in connection with the massacre of a number of Muslim soldiers undergoing secret military training on the island of Corregidor. He was defended by a Maj. Prospero Olivas and was acquitted.

"Today, Colonel Abadilla is one of the principal aides to the same Prospero Olivas, ... the person assigned to investigate the assassination of Aquino."

A left-wing publication, *Liberation*, pointedly commented (and accurately) that Colonel Abadilla owned the major trucking company in the area where General Aguirre (suspected of telling Aquino about a possible plot) was side-swiped by a hit-and-run truck and killed.

With all the conflicts in statements even among the top officers in charge and the obvious attempts to straighten out their stories after the fact, what was the plan? Keep Aquino on the plane and ship him out; take him over to AVSECOM and have Custodio find his papers were not in order and then put him back on the airplane; or pack him off to his old cell at Fort Bonifacio?

President Marcos proferred an explanation in an interview reported by the *San Francisco Examiner's* Phil Bronstein on September 9: The first order from General Ver to check his papers on the plane could not take place because of the confusion on the plane as it landed and lack of information as to when the plane was leaving again made the plan impossible. The contingency plan according to Marcos was to take him to Philippine air force headquarters to "protect him," by placing him in his old prison cell at Fort Bonifacio.

At the same press conference Marcos tried out a double theory of motivation on the assassination: "deepest kind of personal hatred" for Aquino, "manipulated by the communists. This is the best story that I personally can think of right now."

Two weeks after Aquino's slaying Ver, Olivas, Custodio, and President Marcos were all voicing the same version: Aquino was going back to his cell in Fort Bonifacio on the death penalty conviction.

Then why the confusion? The answer was that none of these contingency plans – or their superficial details – really mattered.

There was a fourth contingency plan: Kill Senator Aquino at the airport.

CHAPTER 18

Testimony Under Oath

A newly-constituted commission to investigate the Aquino assassination was finally seated and held its first formal hearing on November 3. The group differed substantially from the Fernando Commission which had disbanded four weeks earlier in that it was made up of five prominent citizens from various walks of life, who were not political insiders from the Marcos administration.

Chairing the new panel was a former Appeals Court Justice, Corazon Agrava. Joining her were educator Amado Dizon, businessman Dante Santos, labor leader Ernesto Herrera, and attorney Luciano Salazar. Appointed general counsel was a former law school dean, Andres R. Narvasa. Narvasa promptly announced that the board had decided to allow cross-examination by qualified attorneys, to permit radio and television coverage, and to keep the hearing public unless a witness objected.

Chairperson Agrava announced that the proceedings would be expedited "within the constraints" placed on the commission. Despite this pledge of speed, the initial session was a meaningless meeting at Camp Crame where Galman's mother hysterically identified his body (although she had done so for the military previously), as did "undercover agent" Rosendo Cawigan and Lt. Col Arturo Custodio.

While the commission was assembling a staff, it took routine testimony on NBI autopsy procedures. So laborious and cautious

157

was the questioning in the early going, that one observer was reported as predicting it would be two years before the hearings were completed.

The deposed chief of AVSECOM, Brig. Gen. Luther Custodio appeared before the panel on November 17. He repeated by rote the claim that the military did not know which plane would carry Aquino or which would be the arrival gate. At that point general counsel Narvasa reached out and pulled a sketch of Gate 8 from the file Custodio was holding in his hand.

General Custodio then admitted that the sketch attorney Narvasa was holding had been part of the security plan, but he "did not fully notice" the sketch at the time he approved Operation Balikbayan.

The beleaguered General could not explain the reason the surveillance cameras—one of which was mounted on a pole directly above the tarmac at Gate 8—did not pick up the assassination on their remote controlled 180-degree wide angle lens. When Narvasa stated that General Olivas had told him that the surveillance cameras had focused on the China airliner's tail section, Custodio could not explain that fact.

Olivas' statements to Narvasa came after an opposition Assemblyman Felimon Fernandez of Cebu had contended that there existed closed-circuit videotapes of the assassination. Even the existence of the cameras had been ignored until a reporter for the *Weekly Guardian*, one Rey Bagatsing, had spotted the cameras following the assassination.

Custodio testified that at the time of the assassination he and his deputy, Col. Romeo Ochoco, were monitoring the two television screens of the surveillance cameras at their central control office but saw nothing of the assassination. He also repeated the story of General Ver's final switch of orders to an outright arrest of Aquino, stating that Ver placed the telephone call changing orders at 6 a.m. the day of the assassination.

Having had surveillance cameras at all nine gates with flights arriving from Asia, Custodio claimed that no taping was made of any one of the surveillance television films since he did not know which gate would receive Aquino.

AVSECOM operations officer, Col. Ager Ontog stated that the security plans and drawings had been focused on Gate 8, but he did not know the reason. Col. Ontog also noted that he did not think security people would let Galman through in the ill-fitting, unzipped clothing he was wearing at the time of his death.

On the 19th the Commission went to Manila International Airport to see for itself how the surveillance system worked. There they watched the landing of a China Airlines plane at Gate 8 and were able to observe on the surveillance system the landing, taxiing and berthing at Gate 8. Only the mid-portion of the side stairway was obscured from the camera, and the foot of the stairs was in view.

General counsel Narvasa said that the two men who operated the system, Ildefonso Flores and Ernesto Torres, would be interviewed.

Custodio also stated that his aide, Lt. Castro, was to have accompanied Aquino to his office as a courtesy, but when asked why he did not, Custodio replied "it would be better if Lt. Castro answered that."

AVSECOM Colonel Ontog was back on the stand on the 24th. He said the killing of Galman was an "overreaction" by the security men. He also said there were four ramp guards at the foot of the stairway used by the Aquino escorts, but they were asked to step backwards out of the way.

The commission was upset by the fact that a Philippine Airlines employee named Jose Orias had been interviewed on local television and in *Bulletin Today* instead of coming before the panel. Orias had said he was delivering a message to the cockpit of the Royal Brunei airliner at the next gate when he looked out the window and saw Galman "hit" Aquino from behind. He also said he later saw Galman lying in a "pool of blood" after the van had pulled away.

The other Custodio, Lt. Col Arturo of the intelligence service, also appeared and told his story of his friendship with Galman. He said he did not know why Galman was arrested by the military in 1982, but he knew it was on orders of President Marcos.

Sgt. Rolando deGuzman, mentioned in the Olivas report as an eyewitness and the first to fire on Galman, testified on November 24. He recalled that he had been sitting in the AVSECOM van with 10 other members of the ALFA squad looking through a crack in the doors which were slightly ajar. When Aquino, with deMesa and Lat holding him, was about three feet away, deGuzman testified, "a man suddenly materialized behind former Senator Aquino, pointing his gun and simultaneously firing it."

"I first hit him with a .45 caliber pistol on his head, and then as he was falling down, I fired six more shots at him." He also testified he did not mean to kill him, although they had orders to shoot to kill anyone who tried to harm Aquino.

"I was not able to warn Aquino or his guard; my first reaction was to draw my gun and shoot Galman once in the head. There was no way I could have shouted a word of warning to Aquino or his guards as Galman immediately fired."

DeGuzman testified that Lat (not deMesa as the Olivas report stated) parried Galman's hand and turned him. That was when the first shot at Galman's head was fired, according to the sergeant. The Olivas report had merely stated that deGuzman fired at the assailant.

S. Sgt. Ernesto Mateo, also a member of the ALFA team in the van testified on the 29th. Mateo said that he did not see the assassination from within the van, but he heard a shot and upon hearing more gunfire leaped from the van.

"When I saw Sgt. deGuzman firing at the gunman, I also fired because I saw him still moving. I was afraid that he might harm Senator Aquino again." Wearing a sharpshooter's badge at the hearing, Sergeant Mateo said that he pumped nine shots from his M16 into Galman between the navel and groin from a distance of about eight feet.

Contrary to deGuzman's testimony, Mateo said that the team was under orders to shoot any attacker but not kill him. He said he fired because Galman was "twitching," but he did not recall seeing any gun.

By examining still photos Mateo placed himself squarely as one of those firing shots that came some 20 seconds after the first four.

Sgt. Rudolfo Desolong identified himself as the leader of the men inside the AVSECOM van, but did not see the assassination.

The New York Times reported on deGuzman's testimony:

> The sergeant said he fired at the assailant even as another soldier shoved him, causing the gunman to fall and drop his weapon. Asked to demonstrate how the gunman fell in relation to the van, his demonstration differed significantly from the scene suggested by still pictures of the actual scene taken by news photographers...
>
> Neither Sergeant deGuzman nor his superiors could explain why they did not get out of the van to help protect Mr. Aquino and did not open the door of the van until after they heard the shooting.
>
> Some lawyers in Manila have suggested that the closed van might have held Mr. Galman, who was then pushed onto the scene at the instant Mr. Aquino was shot from behind by one of his guards, and that it seems improbable that a van sent to drive Mr. Aquino away should have had its doors closed...

DeGuzman's testimony did not match the pattern of shots found on the sound tracks. The initial burst of gunfire that felled Galman included only four shots. The sergeant claimed to be the first to hit him, and contended that he shot him in the back of the head as Galman spun around from a push by Lat (instead of deMesa). That last discrepancy from the official version indicated that he did not see Aquino shot at all. Apparently deGuzman was the man in the photographs leaning out firing his .45 into the prostrate Galman some 20 seconds after the four shots that downed him. He could not have shot Galman in the head with his pistol.

Mateo's testimony that he commenced firing when deGuzman stopped meshed with the actual scenario shown on film. Thus, Sgt. Mateo was the man who riddled the corpse with a rapid fire blast from his M16, and he could point to photographs to prove it.

Therefore, in reality, deGuzman began firing 20 seconds after Galman had been hit and Mateo followed him. So deGuzman's claim of being the first to shoot Galman, and the attempt to explain the wound in the back of the head, was so much perjury. Whether deGuzman devised his story to ingratiate himself with his superiors or he was coached cannot be determined.

Had deGuzman and Mateo pumped all the shots into the front of Galman that they claimed to have, there ought to have been more signs of wounds and blood on the front of his clothes. The most plausible explanation of why there was not is that his heart had stopped pumping much earlier.

By the beginning of December, the commission was talking about obtaining the Japanese videotapes, calling Wakamiya, trying to get the testimony of two unidentified Filipino women who a Japanese legislator claimed were eyewitnesses to the military killing of Aquino, and calling military people to explain how Galman ended up on his back if he were shot in the back of the head.

It was more than 100 days since Ninoy Aquino had died.

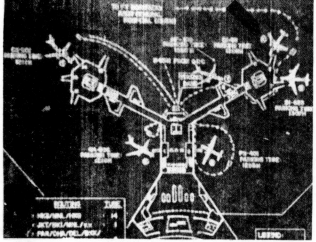

Fig. 6. Military Plan for August 21 (note route of van at Gate 8).

CHAPTER 19

A Matter of Succession

Almost from the moment of Senator Aquino's death, President Marcos, Imelda Marcos and General Olivas had attributed the motive for the killing to either communists wishing to eliminate a moderate rival and embarrass the government or personal revenge. Sometimes the trio got the possible motives logically confused: a man willing to sacrifice his own life (to explain how he was able to charge up to the guards) or a "notorious killer-for-hire," were not compatible theories.

The Cawigan fantasy was used by Marcos to support the communist killer hypothesis. The government's supposed inquiry into the deaths of several witnesses at Aquino's military trial was intended to support a vengeance explanation. This was a favorite of Imelda's which at one point she embellished by a story that there was an anonymous man who wanted revenge because Ninoy had raped his wife.

If Galman was hired to kill Aquino for either ideological (subversive) or personal (revenge) reasons, he had to have an escape route so he could spend the money he had earned. If the government version is to be believed, he was given no way out and he did not bother to put up a fight.

These hypothetical motives – so casually bandied about by the apologists for the government's story – would make no sense if the military were responsible instead of Galman.

Once Galman was removed from the formula, so would be

the claim that the killer was hired by subversives or by some lone person with a grudge.

The obvious motive was to remove Benigno Aquino as an impediment to succession to the Presidency of the Philippines. Aquino was more than an opposition leader, and more than an able politician. He not only had the intelligence and dynamism to make him a popular vote-getter, but he was a living symbol of a return to democracy, of electoral and economic reform, and of peace and a national reconcilation. With Aquino in the presidential chair the leaders under the Marcos regime would not just have been defeated, their system of authoritarian rule and personal aggrandizement would have been destroyed.

Despite Marcos' complaint to ABC's Sam Donaldson that the western media had "created" Aquino as the leader of the opposition, the Senator was the leader and a lot more. Ninoy had the love of millions, and the respect of other leaders, such as the Laurels, Tanada, Diokno, Rodrigo, Pimentel, expatriate Senators Salonga, Manglapus, Osmena, and the other exiled leaders, young activists, one-time Liberal President Macapagal, and such disillusioned Nationalist party people as deposed Vice President Fernando Lopez. Doy Laurel, as Chairman of the united opposition, UNIDO, was prepared to move forward with Aquino in the lead.

In a practical vein, Aquino was an excellent political organizer and dynamic campaigner.

The motive for his elimination, simply put, was succession to the Presidency and the political and economic power that went with it. If Aquino came home, his death was mandatory if there was going to be political power after Marcos.

Columnist Jack Anderson on September 22, 1983, Paul Quinn-Judge, of the *Christian Science Monitor* on September 7, 1983, and two leftist Filipino academics in Berkeley, California, Joel Rocamora and Barbara Cort in "The Philippines After Aquino, After Marcos?" published by the Philippine Support Committee and the Southeast Asia Resource Center, October,

1983 all reached the conclusion that presidential succession was the motive.

The succession issue had been around since 1971, but somehow Ferdinand Marcos had always arranged for Ferdinand Marcos to succeed himself. He declared martial law, he got a constitutional assembly to change the constitution to the way he wanted it and he set up an interim assembly to conduct an election he could not lose. But now the game had changed. Marcos' health was deteriorating in an irregular rate of decline due to a recurring kidney problem. The economy was staggering. Marcos had devalued the peso twice, and funding from the International Monetary Fund (IMF) was needed to bail him out for the time being. Pressured by a population increasingly restive under authoritarianism, Marcos' machinery called a presidential election in 1987. Death, defeat or retirement for Marcos was no longer in the unforeseeable future.

President Marcos – even after 18 years in office – was not a disinterested party. Quite to the contrary, determining who followed him was of prime importance to him. Living in retirement, he would want a Marcos loyalist to succeed him so that he and his family could preserve what they had amassed, both in material wealth and political influence.

Even facing impending death, Marcos would be concerned with his place in history. Would he be remembered as a forceful leader who only used martial law out of necessity to bring order and improvement to the Philippines, or would he become a sad footnote remembered for tyranny and personal plunder? His successor could lead a nation in weeping upon his death or be the first Filipino to breathe a national sigh of relief at his passing. It is virtually inbred among successful politicians to protect their historical role as their heritage, their share of immortality.

To guarantee favorable treatment of him and his memory, Marcos' successor had to be someone who would extol the name of Ferdinand Marcos and keep intact what had passed for the "New Society" movement.

Yet that analysis – shared by many Filipino intellectuals – was really too cerebral. The source of Marcos' determination to be the guiding hand in selecting his successor was more emotional. At heart Marcos is a gut fighter, a survivor by fair means or foul, who operates by his own rules and own determination to get his, to keep his, and to make sure no one takes it from him and his.

Because of this attitude, it is not surprising that in the maneuvering for the annointment of a successor, President Marcos turned away from three advisors who had intellectual credentials, in favor of those who were not only loyal to him, but were of the same gut fighter instincts.

Smooth, handsome Minister of Defense Juan Ponce Enrile – the one time favorite – has slipped so far in influence that Marcos told a *London Observer* reporter shortly before Aquino's death that "The Minister of Defense is nowhere in the chain of command. He cannot even order a single battalion from Cagayan of Ilocos." Enrile's loyalty is overshadowed by his personal friendships with the elite in the opposition. This has made him a ready target for his enemies within the administration, to the extent that it was reported that he feared for his life.

Also sliding down the influence pole has been West Point graduate, General Fidel Ramos, the most professional of the top army officers. Head of the Philippine Constabulary – the home army and federal police force – within the past year, much of Ramos' authority was transferred by Marcos edicts to General Fabian Ver, the man Marcos appointed Chief of Staff of the Armed Forces in August, 1981.

Prime Minister Cesar Virata probably had never been a succession player, except that in the event of Marcos' death or disability – pursuant to the latest version of the constitution – he would be interim head of state while the nation was being run by a 15-man "executive committee." A skilled economist, the Prime Minister crossed swords with Imelda Marcos on budgetary matters and thus further weakened his position at the Presidential palace. His statement immediately after the assassination that "the military may have had a hand in it" was remarkable for its candor.

Fabian Ver is a Marcos relative, whose rise is from chauffeur and bodyguard for Marcos to Chief of Staff is due entirely to the President. The General owes everything to Marcos, who in turn has depended on Ver in recent years as his liaison to control the military. Ver has also filled a special need in an administration fraught with paranoia on the one hand and employing "hard ball" tactics on the other. He has long headed the Security Unit of the Armed Forces. It is this group, in its various forms and apparently separate units (now including AVSECOM) which often has been identified by the opposition (and such organizations as Amnesty International) as the perpetrators of murders, tortures and other human rights violations. As a possible successor Ver fits three qualities admired by Marcos: Unswerving loyalty, mean-toughness, and survival at any cost.

Imelda Marcos, has been mentioned often as having ambitions to succeed her husband. She has been at Marcos' side from his days as a rising Congressman. Often his spokesperson when the iron hand in the velvet glove or beauty and charm were prerequisites, she has been credited with having a significant role in Marcos' decisions. There is a popular Filipino joke: "What do we do if our leader dies?" "I guess President Marcos will have to run things by himself."

The once poor relative to the ne'er-do-well branch of the Roumaldez family, Imelda knows what it means to fight her way to the top rung and stay there. In addition to political power she has a tremendous amount to protect since she and her relatives acquired extensive business interests during the martial law period. Although possibly hampered in any succession battle by being a woman, she is not nick-named "The Iron Butterfly" for nothing.

Marcos built up his wife's administrative credentials by appointing her Governor of Metro Manila, naming her Minister of Human Settlements, giving her several diplomatic missions, and in 1982 placing her on the 15-person Executive Committee. After Aquino's death she told a group of foreign correspondents she was tired of politics and in November she resigned from the Executive Committee. Many Imelda watchers think this is a ploy to step back in order to eventually step forward. She may have been shocked by the great public reaction to Aquino's death and not want the Presidency for herself. It is unlikely that she would voluntarily relinquish a voice in the selection of a successor. Nor would Imelda want to be without influence in any future administration. She has much to protect and like her husband she is concerned with both her place in history and worldly possessions.

However, there is another player in the succession sweepstakes. His name: Eduardo Cojuangco, Jr. Cojuangco heads the coconut monopoly which Marcos has allowed him to operate without interference. He is also in control of the United Coconut Planters Bank in the Makati financial district. Until it appeared that Defense Minister Enrile was losing ground in the succession infighting, Cojuangco had been Enrile's top financial backer. But early in 1983 Cojuangco switched allegiance to the Ver/Imelda faction, and sealed the deal with a financial coup. In March he was permitted by the government to purchase 20 percent of the stock of the San Miguel Beer Company – the Philippines largest corporation – from Enrique Zobel, who had a disagreement with company management. In exchange the chairman of San Miguel was able to buy a large block of United Coconut Planters Bank shares.

A financial transaction of that size could not happen without Marcos' personal approval since all such stock permits are subject to his sanction – and sometimes require participation of favorites or himself.

Long involved in politics, there is little left for a man of Cojuangco's ambition and manipulative skill, except the presidency. He could let Ver and Imelda have their turn and then by the end of the decade it would come to him. If it was too difficult for Ver or Imelda to take the presidency themselves, it might fall to him directly.

Cojuangco's profile would be incomplete without mention of several special facts. He is the first cousin of Aquino's widow, Corazon; he had an abiding hatred for Ninoy. According to Paul Quinn-Judge, *Christian Science Monitor*, September 7, 1983, he provided some of the witnesses against Aquino at the latter's military trial; several union organizers in the coconut plantations he controlled met violent deaths. Coincidentally, one Emmanual Pelaez, although a pro-Marcos politician, nevertheless criticized the coconut monopoly in 1982. Shortly thereafter Pelaez was shot by a person or persons unknown and almost died.

Contrary to the repeated claims of Marcos that the communists had the most to gain from the death of Senator Aquino, the person who had the most to benefit was Ferdinand Marcos.

CHAPTER 20

Manilagate: The Conspiracy

Sometime in the three days before Sunday, August 21, a final decision was made by the conspirators to have Senator Aquino assassinated at the airport.

The radically-oriented newspaper *Liberation* published a story in November which claimed Salvador Laurel had received a telephone call from an anonymous businessman who contended that the assassination plot had been hatched in the banking offices of Eduardo Cojuangco, Jr., head of the coconut monopoly, back in June with President Marcos giving tacit approval. Supposedly involved were two aides of Cojuangco, the head of the coconut monopoly, as well as General Fabian Ver and a Colonel Mejia. While potentially true, it was unlikely that even if such a meeting took place it resulted in the final plan. In the first place the tip was by an unnamed informer and therefore was automatically suspect. How would the tipster have discovered the details of a meeting on such a sensitive matter as high-level murder, any more than Cawigan would have, if he had not been present?

In June the government was using every means imaginable to keep Aquino from coming home and most of the Marcos people did not seriously think he would come; they believed his planned return was a propaganda ploy.

But the best evidence that the actual assassination plan was developed in the week after Aquino left the United States was the change in signals from General Ver and certain loose ends that marred the smooth operation of the conspiracy.

If controlling the succession to the Presidency and maintenance of the authoritarian power of the Marcos regime were the motives, then Aquino's death made a great deal of sense to anyone willing to consider murder as a political means. Aquino's imminent arrival at Manila International Airport forced the conspirators to make a rapid assessment of their options:

1. Keep him on the airliner, show that his "papers" were either false or non-existent, and ship him right back to the point of embarkation. Strength: It would keep him out of the country at least for a time – perhaps until President Reagan completed his visit. Weaknesses: Aquino would undoubtedly try again. Challenging the travel papers of a Filipino citizen supposedly only on humanitarian release might make the government look foolish since the documentation had been withheld from him by the very government which was trying to make him a "non-person." This would not eliminate him as a political force.

2. Have President Marcos go through the motions of greeting Aquino as an old, but respected rival and then place him under some form of house arrest. Advantage: It might discredit Ninoy with some of the more radical elements. Weaknesses: It would make the military tribunal conviction look like a mockery. Aquino would be free to organize and direct the opposition campaign. As a living symbol of reform and the return of democracy he would be in a very strong position to weld together most of the opposition if given regular access to the leadership.

3. Arrest Aquino and put him back in a cell at Fort Bonifacio. According to Ver, Marcos, Olivas and Custodio this was the government's official position, although it was several days after his death before all of them were singing the same tune. Advantage: He would be less able to organize and build up enthusiasm. Weaknesses: This would create sympathy for Aquino internationally and would become the focus of claims of human rights violations, political imprisonment, and other

174

complaints. The conspirators, remembering the 1978 election for the interim assembly and Aquino's moral power from behind bars, would not welcome this solution.

4. Suggest Marcos carry out the death sentence by "musketry" as ordered by the military court and as Marcos had indicated could still occur. This was unthinkable, since the worldwide as well as the Filipino reaction would have been tremendously adverse to the current regime.

To those who were afraid of Aquino as the stumbling block to presidential ambitions (and those who relied on them for power and monetary gain) all these solutions had inherent disadvantages.

If Aquino could be kept away, then his effort to return could be made to look a bit foolish. He would have to slink back to Newton, Massachusetts, essentially powerless. But if Aquino, like General Douglas MacArthur in another era, could fulfill his promise to return to Philippine soil, the most attractive option was to kill him.

At least some of those willing to consider outright murder undoubtedly had personal reasons for assassination. Aquino was everything some of them were not. He was a happy, honest man, content with his own destiny, born to the elite but naturally popular with the masses, admired, respected. Such a man engenders great trust and love, but also envy and hate. Thus, for them a political execution was not a hard decision.

The greatest potential disadvantage for any conspirators – especially those in the government – was that the conspirators would be found out, disgraced and their futures ruined. The problem would be how to manage the Senator's death while minimizing suspicion and the danger of discovery.

If Aquino were placed in prison and then died from whatever means, ranging from poison to a faked fight, the government would be blamed. This had happened to less famous political prisoners, but the spotlight was on Aquino. Therefore, that option was out.

An attempt on his life while he was in some form of house

arrest, parole or limited freedom would be chancy since Ninoy would be protected by a large number of people around him, including his own bodyguards. Even if successful this option was fraught with messy variables. In any event, providing Aquino any form of freedom in which he could communicate with the public would be unpopular with those who wished Aquino would evaporate.

Having him shot by a sniper away from the airport had two certain disadvantages: 1) the strong possibility of missing; 2) The certainty of blame being placed on the government. Putting Aquino in a position where a sniper would have a sure shot – and a ready means of escape – would be demonstrable proof that he had been set up for death by the government.

Therefore, having discarded the above options, the conspirators must have arrived at the idea of killing him at the airport by a process of elimination.

This plan posed three problems: 1) How to guarantee that he would be killed and forever eliminated? 2) How to do so without blame being automatically placed on the government or the individual conspirators? 3) How to keep the press and public from viewing the murder being committed by agents of the conspirators?

The solution that would guarantee results was to select some trustworthy person or persons who would not miss and would not talk. There were only two types of people who could fit that category: professional gangsters and trained military. Use of criminals created more problems than it solved, ranging from availability to blackmail. Besides, young military men who would be happy to ingratiate themselves could be found close at hand.

To deflect blame away from the government of the conspirators, the appearance had to be given that every effort was being made to protect Aquino – with a great flurry of visible activity, back up paperwork, orders, plans and substantial numbers of people mobilized for the effort.

Equally important was conclusive "proof" that others had committed the murder. This had to go further than merely placing the blame to the actual set up of an identifiable human scapegoat. This man must be believable. He must have an unsavory reputation, a history of violence, criminality, subversive connections, or all of the above. If any pieces of his dreadful background were missing they could be concocted. Unfortunately the scapegoat had to wind up dead to guarantee silence and uncontradicted guilt. In deciding how to accomplish the death of the supposed killer the conspirators had a precedent: When a man ran onto a theater stage and slashed at Imelda Marcos with a bolo knife, her guards shot the attacker dead on the spot. A little overzealous behavior would take care of such a man if he could be found and lured to the scene.

The press and the public could be kept away in the name of security for poor Aquino, who had so many enemies that plots on his life abounded. Already the public knew such threats existed, and President Marcos had sent his wife Imelda to warn him personally, as had Defense Minister Enrile.

A controlled setting was essential to the deed. It would be necessary to pick a location which would be unlikely to be available to casual or accidental observation.

There needed to be a murder weapon which was untraceable to anyone, but which would attract the public's attention.

Be bold. Be quick. Whatever the temporary heat, or the carping of the suspicious or the distraught, Aquino would be removed from the political scene once and for all.

The airport was a controlled situation. Airport Security (AVSECOM) was now under the general staff. Television cameras of the airport belonged to the government and could be neatly censored. All the major daily newspapers were now pro-government – some owned by administration insiders or relatives.

Intimidation would be employed if someone saw something he or she should not have seen and had the indescretion to speak out. If the conspirators would kill a Senator, would they hesitate with an army private, an airport maintenance man, or an unknown passenger?

There would be people accompanying Aquino. A relative,

a friend, a couple of reporters, perhaps. To thwart them – to keep them from seeing what was going on – mislead them as to what was going to happen and then act suddenly, leaving them stranded and blinded from the truth.

Be bold. Be quick. So what if the opposition press – a mere handful of tolerated tabloids: *Mr. & Mrs., Tempo, Malaya, The Paper,* and some others barely more than newsletters – screamed that the government was negligent. Sack a commander, reprimand a few, then reward them later. An admission of human error was worth never having to worry about Ninoy Aquino again.

So the death squad was chosen: Young, tough, ambitious low echelon fellows – many from the home provinces of the conspirators – who could be trusted to tell a simple, single story and never breathe a word of their deadly work. Supervise them with some hard-nosed intelligence agents, who had seen a dirty deed or two in their days. They would be professional and loyal.

Surround them with hundreds of soldiers and agents who need know little or nothing except their assigned tasks set out in a complex operational plan. Send them off in all directions, guarding that, checking this, "securing" something else – with eyes and ears directed outward from the death scene.

Rolando Galman was available as the scapegoat. He had been held in reserve – fed and watered like a steer, never knowing his ultimate fate – for just such an operation. Whether Lt. Col. Arturo Custodio knew – or cared – that he was delivering his erstwhile drinking buddy to a fatal rendezvous may never be known. But lead him he did.

Gate 8 – at the end of a long arm from the main terminal – became the object of great interest to AVSECOM, Metrocom and government intelligence at least two days before Aquino's arrival. Its tube had a flight of metal stairs down to the ground which were out of the line of vision of almost all passengers and from Gate 8 within the terminal.

Aquino had been spotted arriving in Taipei, Taiwan, after

a flight from Singapore. Almost too late for him to find a new taking off point without missing August 21.

The soon-to-be alleged murder weapon had been procured: An untraceable Smith & Wesson .357 magnum revolver, purchased in Springfield, Massachusetts in 1970, and hijacked with a load of weapons just when it arrived in Thailand shortly thereafter. Intelligence agents know where to find such pieces — possibly taken off some dead insurgent or inept strongarm man.

Recruitment and rehearsal of the AVSECOM, Constabulary and security men from the armed forces had been completed and their roles spelled out. But the planning was hasty.

The Ver announcement, repeated as late as Friday morning, that Aquino would be shipped out without leaving the plane was countermanded that Saturday. He would be brought to AVSECOM headquarters at an air base close to the airport; if he had no proper papers he would be deported, but if he entered legally then to Fort Bonifacio. The logical absurdity of that smokescreen must have struck someone during Saturday or after the fact when the hounds of truth started nipping at the conspirators' heels. Thus, a new order was inserted into Olivas' second report that Aquino would be arrested; he was, after all, a paroled murderer according to the government.

An informant at Chiang Kai Chek airport in Taiwan confirmed that Senator Aquino had boarded flight 811.

China flight 811 was coming to a halt at the airport, when the blue AVSECOM van of trusted men pulled onto the tarmac of Gate 8. Plainclothesmen slipped in between a line of baggage trucks. A car was in place under the lip of the terminal building for emergencies. Other squads trotted into position as the airliner taxied to meet the jetway which would take its human cargo into the terminal.

The local television crews, press photographers and a gaggle of reporters were pressed close to the entrance from the jetway where they had been ordered to by an intelligence officer. They had been assured that airport manager Tubuena would shake Aquino's hand when the Senator emerged. Elsewhere a crew from the government's official television station filmed the airliner as it nudged up to the jetway and cut its four engines. In an office commandeered for the day intelligence men watched the action on a series of screens which fed the surveillance cameras placed on towers above each gate.

Up the side stairway came Lat, deMesa, Lazaga and probably Moreno. The first three entered the plane while their leader Lt. Castro (in a barong) stood by the door and Moreno waited in the jetway. Several plainclothesmen, including Sergeant Miranda and an airman in khaki all crowded into the jetway. Several agents, including Castro, entered the plane – and watched while Aquino was arrested.

Lat and deMesa rushed Aquino down the aisle and into the jetway. There they made a sudden left turn out the door to the stairway as Miranda and Moreno swung in behind. Then they headed down the stairway while the doorway was blocked by Castro, several agents and the soldier in khaki. Those probing television cameras and the surprising number of reporters had to be blocked off.

Someone said in Tagalog: "I'll do it."

Sergeant deMesa countered: "I'll do it."

Another voice yelled out: "Here he comes." Whether this was said by someone on the stairs or on the ground was not clear, but a moment later, the same man ordered in the Visayan dialect: "Shoot him."

His words were echoed by another: "Shoot him."

And then came the shot.

Who pulled the trigger?

At first blush, Sergeant deMesa was the most likely suspect. According to the NBI he tested strongly positive for nitrates on the paraffin test. The shot was fired at close range at the left side of Aquino where deMesa was holding Aquino in a vice-like grip of his powerful right hand. But he was probably not the actual assassin for several reasons: First, although he apparently offered to kill at the head of the stairs, it is not certain what "do it" meant. Secondly, deMesa had his right hand full of Aquino's arm. It would be virtually impossible for him to loosen his grip and draw a pistol from some hidden place, since he was not wearing a holster.

If the first call of "Pusila" (Shoot him) had come from one of those on the stairway, then Miranda, as the ranking agent probably gave the order. There was a pattern to the interchanges, as illustrated in the sonogram: "C" called out "Here he is" and "B" repeated it. "C" ordered "Shoot him" and "B" echoed the command. If "C" were a voice from some unknown agent waiting on the ground – and it would be likely since the ramp guards had to be ordered to turn around, then Miranda was a strong possibility since he would not have given the order.

Lazaga, also behind Aquino, was a hesitant sort. When Kashiwahara demanded to accompany Aquino, Lazaga stood by helplessly until deMesa told the brother-in-law to "take seat." He was hard to picture as a trigger man; he was not assertive, he was a follower.

According to the government version, 14 men were given the paraffin test and, of those, four were in the group coming down the stairs. If the NBI report was to be believed one of the escorts descending the stairs was not tested. In all likelihood that would have been Miranda since he was not in the official escort group. He wore a loose borong under which it would be easy to hide a pistol stuck in his belt, where under normal procedures the plainclothes agents carry their .45s.

Miranda was particularly interesting because he had an escape route. He hid under the jetway for about 40 seconds – Aquino's bag in his hand – and then ran directly to a waiting car, snuggled in under the upper floor of the terminal.

It is impossible to know for sure, since the government might not tell the truth about the paraffin tests, or the order in which the men were on the stairs. In the re-enactment, neither Miranda nor Moreno appeared at all. In real life either of them, or Lazaga could have reached forward and fired downward into Aquino's neck.

Considering the enormity of the crime, the finger on the trigger was not the vital issue, but who ordered the deed.

Immediately after the death shot which had to have taken place at the foot of the stairs, deMesa and Lat threw the body of Senator Aquino forward onto the tarmac so as to place him where an alleged killer might have come up behind them.

And the unlucky Rolando Galman, how did he arrive on the scene? There were 3.5 seconds between the shot into Aquino's neck and the burst of four. Galman wound up on his back even closer to the van than did Aquino. Looking at all the photographs which included the van and the chart which lays out the entire scene, there were only two places Galman could have been— either in the van or hidden behind it. Except for a theoretical race from under the plane past a dead Aquino just in time to be shot, there was no other cover within the 3½ seconds necessary to reach his final location.

This would account for reporter Ueda's placing Galman as standing there "at a loss" in front of Aquino, and would attest to reporter Wakamiya's disputed version of the man pushed from the van. It would not be in conflict with the West German passenger Albath's description of events.

The autopsy of Galman told of half-digested rice in his stomach which would indicate he ate a light lunch before coming to the scene. He had to have been brought to Gate 8 by whomever he was working for, to play whatever role he thought was his.

Two facts about Galman have to be reconciled. The first is the existence of the bullet wound in the back of the head behind the ear. The second is that in the photo of the dead Galman lying on his back on the ground his blood appears to have run "up" his forehead and cheeks from the wound in the back of the head, contrary to the law of gravity. The only possible explanation of the latter phenomenon is that at some time *after* the shot in the head he had been lying on his stomach when the blood would run *down* toward the front of his face.

Sergeant deGuzman for the first time in mid-November

claimed that one of the seven shots he took at Galman hit him in the head. But the fact was that deGuzman's story did not add up since according to the sound track and the "ear" witnesses only four shots were fired in the first volley. Two of these — from deGuzman or whomever – hit Galman in the back. Even if it were postulated that the first shot landed in the back of his head it would not account for the blood dripping up his face.

Galman had to have been shot in the back of the head *before* being pushed forward as a living vegetable. Whether this premature disposition of Galman was due to his becoming obstreperous upon sensing something was wrong or just a simpler means of handling matters was best known to ALFA team. A careful look at the photos of Galman prostrate on the ground shows that his trouser fly was partially unzipped and his belt appeared to be loose. Why this was so was a matter of surmise, but one answer would be that his "maintenance man" garb was put on him after he had been overpowered or shot. Whether the first shot to his head was fired before or after he got in the van cannot be determined.

Since the first shot quite likely was delivered before he was sent out on the tarmac, it is equally probable that he wound up on his back because one of the first four shots came from in front of him tossing him backward. Two shots on the sound track were nearly simultaneous, suggesting a second shooter. That single bullet probably came from someone placed under the plane or off to the side, at least equidistant from the microphones as the three shots from the van.

If deGuzman or some other AVSECOM man fired at Galman from the van, their victim would have to have been facing toward where Aquino had fallen since both bullets entered the back.

The story of the Smith & Wesson magnum revolver, complete with lots of pictures, has been told so often in such detail, that almost all analysts have only questioned whether it was the murder weapon. In all probability it was never at the tarmac near Gate 8 at all.

The government eyewitnesses on the scene universally are not telling the truth since it was impossible for Galman to be the lone assassin. The independent eyewitnesses' memories, although fleeting, partial and at time confused, described him with no mention of a gun. Sergeant deMesa told a strange tale invented after the reenactment of running over and picking up the gun. In the government re-enactment, he just plain ran away. DeMesa said he gave the .357 Magnum to another AVSECOM man, who unfortunately had testified that he had run and hid and never mentioned the Smith & Wesson. In the first reports of shells and casings on the scene no mention was made of the deformed magnum shell, but Olivas later produced one for testing. Only General Olivas' word places it near the death scene. He certainly did not display the shell at the press conference at 5:15 on August 21, although General Custodio held up the much handled magnum as the death weapon.

Why did deGuzman, Mateo and perhaps a couple of other AVSECOM men—who waited an unexplained 15 to 20 seconds to come out of the van—fire so many shots into the corpse of Rolando Galman? Certainly not as was so naively testified by Mateo, to see that he did Senator Aquino no further harm. Galman was through. There was no gun in sight. If there had been some real concern, the sharpshooters of ALFA would have sprung into action much sooner.

The answer is simple: There needed to be so many gunshots and so many bullet holes in Galman that witnesses would be confused and, more importantly, any investigation or autopsy would not be able to determine the sequence of wounds, including the earlier shot in the back of the neck.

Who was involved in the implementation and direction of the conspiracy to murder Benigno Aquino? The inquiry must begin literally and figuratively at the trigger finger, and work back through the arm, shoulder and eventually to the brain of the conspiracy. Obviously, whoever actually fired the fatal shot, the five men on the stairway—deMesa, Lat, Lazaga, Miranda and Moreno – were at the trigger end of the plot. They were a mix of AVSECOM and Metrocom soldiers.

These five were under the supervision of 2d. Lt. Jesus Castro, who normally was an aide to General Custodio, head of AVSECOM until relieved of duty shortly after the killing. The Metrocom participants were under the command of General Prospero Olivas, who not only ordered the apparent plan to protect Aquino, but has been in charge of the military investigation of the crime.

The ten men of ALFA squad in the AVSECOM van had to be knowing participants in the operation since they arranged for Galman to wind up on the tarmac from whatever source. They also participated in several ways which would make the plot work and the government version saleable. In addition there were other AVSECOM men and white-shirted agents on the scene, including the uniformed men seen running away in Wakamiya's first picture, the unconcerned agent who returned to the jetway even before the shooting stopped and the agents who forcefully covered the television lenses.

Several other security agents from AVSECOM and the general staff had to know at least enough to fulfill their functions in the scenario of death. These would include Colonel Vicente Tigas of National Intelligence and security and Romeo Bautista who kept the television and cameramen bunched together out of camera range at the jetway exit to Gate 8.

Several of the men from the other AVSECOM squads positioned around the plan knew enough of the conspiracy to give false testimony. Others chose to have seen nothing since they were busy looking for infiltrators on the scene.

Colonel Rolando Abadilla, chief of the Military Intelligence and Security Group of Metrocom, was part of the action, not because of his notorious reputation, but for solid reasons. He was present with General Olivas to support the story of the General's "find" of the old identification badge on Galman's death. Abadilla was also in a position to provide this fortuitous piece

185

of evidence for Olivas. Galman did not slip through security with that ID. How simple for Abadilla to note that many months before one of his men had reported a lost ID, and then to have one produced. Since Galman did not have it, Abadilla was the obvious source.

General Custodio, head of AVSECOM, had to be a principal expediter of the plot. Too many of the active participants were under his direct orders. His aide, Castro, supervised the taking of Aquino on the airliner and directed the blocking of the doorway. It was Custodio, and not the higher-ranking General Olivas, who was the conduit for General Ver's supposed changes in orders.

General Prospero Olivas, Metrocom Chief, was part and parcel of the immediate planning, and along with Custodio created the image of the tremendous amount of security activity at the airport. His men were involved as part of the "close-in" security, which carried out the assassination. They would not have done so without his orders. Olivas' central role afterwards, including the unhesitating appointment as chief investigator by General Ver on the afternoon of the killing, puts him right in the middle of the conspiracy.

As for the other Custodio, Lt. Col. Arturo Custodio, of General Ver's security staff, it was he who directly or indirectly channeled Galman into the arena of security work. Whether he was privy to the plot to the assassination, thereafter he certainly fitted his conduct to the government version. He went to the point of making himself look a bit like a hard-drinking incompetent, while trying to link Galman to subversives.

As for airport manager Tabuena, it was probably not necessary to make him aware of the plot, just as long as he followed orders and kept his suspicions to himself. This was undoubtedly also true of many others who felt unease about what was happening around them.

Although General Fidel Ramos was in command of the Philippine Constabulary, and thus, technically Olivas' chief, he did not have to be part of the plot. By personality and West Point training he would have been an unlikely participant. His position had been eroded gradually by the increasing influence and actual authority of General Ver. He was quick to be critical of the "security" at the airport, but that could be a blind.

General Fabian Ver? Paul Quinn-Judge of the *Christian Science Monitor* quotes unidentified military officers: "Ver may not have known, but he more likely did." The thrust of their story was that Aquino was shot much as has been described here, but that the assassination might have been directed by Colonels like Abadillo and his friend, Arturo Custodio.

The problem with any thesis that this was carried out without Ver's approbation is that he participated publicly in several particulars: He gave Olivas the broad investigatory powers immediately after the assassination and he made the change in posture from keeping Aquino on the plane to placing him where he could be shot. Any junior officers who carried forth such a conspiracy on their own, involving so many people, would eventually become known to General Ver, who headed all security and intelligence operations in the armed forces.

But most of all, Ver was one of the those who had a motive as well as the power.

The real remaining question is whether the plot stopped with Fabian Ver or involved others at the highest level of government and the Philippine power structure.

Only the cover up of the conspiracy to kill Benigno Aquino remained to be examined for clues.

CHAPTER 21

Manilagate: The Coverup

If the assassination conspiracy was bold, the attempt to conceal the true story of the murder of Benigno Aquino, Jr. was equally ambitious.

It did not require much deductive reasoning to determine that the cover up scenario was an integral part of the conspirators' original calculations. The heart of the plan was to give the world a fictitious but believable picture of the crime.

When the smoke had cleared, Senator Aquino would lie dead. His assailant, a gun for hire with subversive connections, would also be dead, shot by the somewhat careless but brave men of AVSECOM. The murder weapon would be recovered. Metrocom and AVSECOM soldiers would be seen on guard to make sure no confederates of the killer were around.

Any witnesses to the contrary would be frightened, intimidated, confused or inaccurate. No Filipino who valued his life would dare contradict the military, especially when the official story was so definitive.

For a period the public's interest in details of Aquino's slaying would be satisfied by announcements of efforts to identify the killer, claims that Aquino had a host of personal enemies, attempts to trace the murder weapon, interviews with "eyewitnesses," autopsies, ballistic tests and all the paraphernalia of a thorough criminal investigation.

That would take care of the evidence and that was the way the story was first presented.

As to motive, much was made of the various warnings that Aquino had received that there was a plot or plots on his life, uncovered by the intelligence unit of the armed forces. Since he ignored these kindly admonitions, Aquino was really responsible for his own death according to the scenario.

Whether by instinct or involvement, President Ferdinand Marcos led the way into the coverup. In statements the night of Aquino's death he theorized on the assassin being willing to give his own life, noted the failure of Aquino to heed warnings, stated the firmness of the President's resolve to uncover any confederates of the alleged assassin, and hinted of probable communist responsibility. This was all in line with the official version of the crime.

If the effort was to foreclose any dispute as to the facts of the killing, again the President fit the pattern three days later. *The Times-Journal* of Manila quoted him: "I have no doubt whatsoever about the fact that they (the media) cannot conceal a very clear fact and that is, that Aquino was shot by a civilian with one single shot with a .357 magnum at close range."

If the conspirators had hoped that suspicions of the military or other government involvement would be contained neatly, they were to be disappointed. If they planned that the responses to nasty questions would come from a single authoritative voice, General Olivas, with support from the presidential palace, then the apparent plan did not go as scheduled.

Foreign journalists, Japanese television cameramen, and bereaved supporters of Aquino began to raise questions which would not go away.

Within a few days after the assassination apologists for the government's version were forced to begin a series of improvisations in a cacophony of voices.

When Japanese crime experts, and anyone who could plot an angle on a graph, began asking about the downward trajectory of the bullet and its possible origin from the stairway, young

Dr. Munoz, the medico-legal man who had performed Aquino's autopsy, promptly adopted a theory of a deflected bullet.

Galman's death without any apparent attempt to flee in the 3.5 seconds left to him, was answered by the testimony of deMesa (as told by General Olivas) of the push, the spin and the fall of Galman.

The conspirators were right, the memory of witnesses was fleeting. Even experienced war correspondent Ken Kashiwahara thought it took 15 to 20 seconds instead of nine for the first shot to be fired. Others misunderstood what was happening, could not remember if they were in front or in back of someone else, in what order men appeared or scrambled fact and supposition. All of the events would have been a fading blur on humanly imperfect senses, except that the cameras did not lie and the sound of death was forever imprinted on tape.

Ninoy Aquino had believed that the presence of the media was a protection. In one sense he was wrong. Baffled and surprised, the instruments of assassination went about their assigned tasks, trying unsuccessfully to hide their faces and deeds from the probing camera, shouting into the wind where the microphones would not be denied.

But in the long run Senator Aquino was right. While the media would not prevent his murder, it would guarantee that the facts of his death could not be concealed.

After the ABC and TBS cameras revealed that at least five men descended the stairs with Aquino, General Olivas blandly comments that there had been an error in the government's re-enactment since some people were not present. He suggested a new re-creation with the help of foreign newsmen.

General Custodio of AVSECOM and his aide, Lt. Castro, the man in charge of the arrest, claimed that it was a last minute decision to take Aquino down the service stairs instead of into the Gate 8 reception area. Why? Answer: The crowd was "surging forward. That "crowd" was the television cameras, government's official and representatives of the local media. In the second Olivas report it was written that it was so calm at

191

Gate 8 that Captain Bautista had sent two of his men over to Gate 7.

There had to be an explanation for the gap in the videotape of the government television camera – from the time Aquino arrived at the head of the stairs until after Galman was first shot. The answer: The government cameraman took cover at the sound of gunfire. Then why did he stop long before there was any gunfire and run away before Aquino was shot?

Did the surveillance cameras record the event? Answer: They did not normally videotape. Did the men monitoring see anything? Answer: Unfortunately, the camera could not view the stairs and was focused on the tail of the plane at the moment of the shooting. When it was proved that the cameras could view the foot of the stairway, there was no explanation.

Despite the theorizing that Galman was hired by the communists, his extensive rap sheet did not provide a scintilla of evidence of communist connections. So enter Cawigan, who related his tale of infiltration of the highest level of the outlawed communists (although he had publicly testified against them in the Aquino trial) and his identification of Galman ("Commander Bert Ramos") as the preferred hit man, chosen over himself.

When Detective Funimoto and others challenged the .357 as the murder weapon because of the small exit wound in Aquino's chin, General Olivas revealed that a deformed magnum cartridge had been found close by Aquino's body. *Los Angeles Times* correspondent Bob Spector – another of those pesky foreign journalists – questioned how a high velocity bullet could have torn through Aquino's skull and then just drop. There was no response.

A bullet hole in the back of Galman's head similar to Aquino's death wound was a nagging bit of evidence. Sergeant deGuzman of ALFA squad belatedly recollected in November that one of his seven shots had hit Galman in the head as the assassin spun around. But how and why were there only four recorded gun reports on the sound track before Galman fell on his back?

If the .357 Smith & Wesson was the murder weapon, why

192

was it handled so that fingerprinting was impossible? After the re-enactment in which deMesa fled the scene without approaching the fallen Galman, Olivas claimed that deMesa had snatched the gun from the slayer's hand and then hid behind the van. Later deMesa was reported to have given the pistol to a Sergeant Martinez. Martinez, on the other hand, was quoted in the second Olivas report as having run and hid behind a "lug" (base of a pylon) where the television cameras had spotted a man hiding.

The re-activated government television camera spotted an agent in a polo barong running from a hiding place under the jetway to a waiting car with what appeared to be one of Aquino's bags. This embarrassment eventually evoked the admission: that it was Sergeant Miranda—one of the men descending the stairway—who wanted to be able to preserve the contents of the luggage.

When the second Olivas report referred to men as "ramp guards" it became apparent that four men had been assigned to the foot of the stairway. Why didn't they see anything? Answer: They had been ordered to move back and face toward the jetway. But would they not have been staring directly toward the alleged path of Galman?

Why were the several military men—in and out of uniform—so intent on blocking the media view down that stairway? Answer: Lt. Castro and the men with him had their hands full trying to keep the "unruly" crowd of passengers from following through the door.

If the men who took Aquino out of the airliner were unarmed, why did the cameras show that two of them had holsters? Answer: They were unarmed.

Could Sergeant Miranda in a barong have had a pistol under his shirt?

Why would the men assigned to protect such a famous personage be unarmed? Answer: Someone in the plane or in the welcoming crowd (if they went into the terminal) might grab a gun. This was the answer even though the holsters had flaps folded in and snapped shut.

193

The questions were endless and the official government answers increasingly contradictory, either of each other or the known facts.

A major problem for the conspiracy was being tied to a falsehood which required inventive justification. The most obvious – and almost ludicrous example – was the government's contention that it did not know that Aquino was on China flight 811, docking at Gate 8. For almost two months after the assassination the government claimed that nine incoming flights had been checked and that security men had been treating all those airplanes originating in the Orient just as they had Aquino's plane.

On the day of the assassination this supposed activity had been employed as an explanation for the spread of manpower throughout the airport and it was suggested that Galman had tracked down Aquino – by following the AVSECOM van around.

The trouble was that this claim was patently untrue. For at least two days before the landing, all plans – including a map – used in handling Aquino's arrest had centered on Gate 8. Early on the morning of the flight someone from the government-controlled Philippine Airlines had phoned the Taiwanese garrison commander and urged him to take good care of Aquino. The press had been ordered to Gate 8 reception area at 11:30 a.m. Reporters found that no other flight had been boarded and the AVSECOM van only came to Gate 8.

In late November the story was amended. Somehow, the new version ran, while China Airlines flight 811 was in the air there had been confirmation that Aquino was on that plane. Further, the new version went, the military in preparing for the Senator's arrival had used Gate 8 merely as an example. By chance number 8 turned out to be the arrival gate.

More far-reaching in its implications was another key element in the coverup: The story circulated from early June that the intelligence arm of the General Staff had discovered a plot – or plots – on Aquino's life if he returned to the Philippines. No substantive evidence of such a plot existed.

That meant that Imelda Marcos' warning in May was nothing more than a threat intended to dissuade Aquino from returning. It was genteel, polite, but definitely a threat – the iron fist had come out of the velvet glove.

What began as a means to convince Ninoy to stay in the United States became a self-fulfilling prophecy of his Murder.

CHAPTER 22

The View From Malacanang

The most persuasive argument against President Marcos being involved in the conspiracy to kill Senator Aquino was the crudeness and blatancy of the act. Marcos was a shrewd, calculating politician who would not take a gamble for uncertain results. It seemed unimaginable that he would contenance a political murder in a public place while the prisoner was in the hands of the Air Force and Constabulary, both of which are accountable to the President.

Jose Diokno, a prominent member of the opposition and a leading civil rights lawyer, said he doubted Marcos had a hand in the slaying because: "He plays things safe. He would never have had Ninoy killed the way he was. Maybe an 'accident' under house arrest, or 'shot while trying to escape,' but not shot in front of the world's press. That's why I believe that the Army was involved." Academic analysts echoed this sentiment, one of them saying that Aquino was a greater threat to Marcos dead than alive.

It is noteworthy that all these assessments by people who knew Marcos or studied his method of operation talked in terms of "cost accounting" and not humanitarian impulses. The lengthy record of imprisonments, charges of torture and mysterious deaths and disappearances which emerged from the martial law era showed that the President was no political saint. He would

197

reject assassination as a political implement for pragmatic reasons, principally the danger of discovery and blame.

Based on the evidence it could not be denied that Ferdinand and Imelda Marcos, unwittingly or not, participated in the coverup of the actual facts of the assassination. The underlying issue became: Was it just a natural reaction in backing up the the position of his staff and a political need to support the military, or a knowing participation in concealing the truth?

From the day of the slaying, Marcos had always claimed that there was a subversive, communist connection to the killing of Aquino. On occasion he had tempered that statement by saying it was only a theory.

For example, on October 2, the following dialogue took place via satellite on ABC's "This Week with David Brinkley":

Sam Donaldson: "Is it your position and the position of your government that he (Galman) was a Communist and that this assassination was ordered by the general chairman of the Philippine Communist Party?"

Marcos: "This is the best that we can gather so far. We are waiting for evidence which disproves this."

The communists and the foreign media had been favorite targets of Marcos. The "subversives" were blamed for anything that went wrong on the one hand, and the foreign press was often criticised by Marcos for creating "misunderstandings" of his administration, on the other.

Marcos consistently said that the communists ("subversives") had the most to gain from Aquino's death on two grounds: 1) elimination of a rival, and 2) embarrassment of the Marcos government. This theory had a certain logic to it.

When reporter Wakamiya's claim that the security men killed Aquino was published, President Marcos said he suspected the story was deliberately planted by elements of the foreign media to malign his administration and the Filipino people in the eyes of the world. "Things are bad enough as it is, but to falsify news or exaggerate it, is compounding the crime," he was quoted in the *Times-Journal* on August 24.

In the same interview with Donaldson, Marcos charged that the media had created Aquino as his opponent:

"You built him up. You tell him he is my opponent. When did he ever become my opponent? He never was my opponent."

While this kind of talk may have been consistent with the coverup it was also typical of the kind of combative political rhetoric which Marcos had used for years in attempts to reduce the hero of millions to a non-person.

Marcos never diverged from his initial support of the official version of the assassination: Aquino was shot by a lone gunman with the .357 magnum. It would have been unthinkable for him to say anything different, because to do so might be an admission that there was a plot involving the military.

Such an admission could prove weakness on two fronts: either 1) that people in his government had plotted *with* his knowledge. or 2) members of his administration had plotted without his knowledge. The tragic flaw in the second possibility was that such an admission could indicate Marcos' vulnerability at the hands of potentially disloyal people within his own administration.

The appointment of a commission to investigate the assassination which was filled with aging political cronies of Marcos was hotly criticized by the opposition and members of the Aquino family. Two of the most vocal critics were Aquino's widow Corazon (Cory) and his brother Agapito "Butz" Aquino. More significantly, as the critics predicted, the commission would not be independent and would do very little.

When lawsuits were filed challenging the commission on the issue of separation of judicial and executive branches, the commission was permitted to shut down its hearings to await a Supreme Court decision. Such niceties had not been allowed to stand in the way of pledged "speedy" action before, unless Marcos wanted it that way.

Stung by complaints about the make-up of the Fernando Commission, the President's attempt to appoint Jaime Cardinal Sin or some other independent to the commission was obvious window dressing since they were almost sure not to accept. However, offering appointments that are certain to be rejected is a standard political maneuver throughout the world.

Imelda Marcos also promoted the government version of the assassination. On September 19, she was interviewed by the foreign press corps in Manila. She told of trying to dissuade Aquino from coming home during their meeting on May 21. She blamed his friends who "practically bullied him" to return while the government tried to stop or postpone his coming. Adroitly she defended the Fernando Commission by comparing it to the Warren Commission which investigated the death of President. John F. Kennedy.

She also echoed her husband's theme that the press was responsible for some loss of credibility by the government. In regard to the assassination itself she said that "We're dying to know the truth."

Occasionally Marcos went beyond the government's story. During a televised meeting with U.S. Senator Mark Hatfield (Rep.-Ore.), he told the Senator that the guards had tried to protect Aquino "with their bodies." Actually, even by their own accounts, they ran like scared rabbits. Marcos repeated the story that nine planes were entered (although once he referred to six) searching for Aquino, but this he would have heard from Olivas or Ver.

There was one crucial point in the coverup in which President Marcos was not just parroting the line of the government (his government) or following his usual political instincts. He and Imelda created the story of a communist plot on Aquino's life.

Imelda's statement to Ninoy on May 21 that he should not come home because there was a plot or plots on his life was an improvisation. And it was, as Aquino realized, a veiled threat.

It was not the first time Mrs. Marcos had threatened Aquino. As Ninoy releated to Steve Psinakis in New York on December 16, 1980, she accused Aquino of having sent "assassination teams to Manila" and said that they would "do the same."

The official line was developed that the intelligence division of the Armed Forces, headed by General Ver, had received word of a communist plot through an undercover agent. This information, according to official dogma, had been the basis of Imelda's warning to Aquino in May. At one point Marcos became confused, for when he first referred to the upcoming Cawigan story in the September 21 ABC interview, Marcos said they got the report of the plot in "June, July." Those months, of course, would have meant the information came after Imelda's meeting with Aquino in New York.

Marcos said in the ABC interview: "All I know is that sometime in June, July, I was alerted by an intelligence report which went to the fact that we should watch out because there is a conspiracy afoot to kill and assassinate Aquino when he arrives at the airport. This intelligence report came in, according to General Ver, Chief of Staff, from a drop. You know what a drop is – a letter dropped by one of the agents inside the Communist Party."

He went on to say that they had located the agent they had planted among the communists but they were prevented from presenting his evidence by "technicalities." The fact was that the "technicalities" to which he referred were that the hearings of the Fernando Commission had been suspended. The Cawigan story was soon released by the government, technical impediments or not.

Marcos is a very bright man. He must know that Cawigan's tale was concocted. Marcos' knowledge of the details of "the drop" mentioned the first time in September did not date back to June or July. It if had, he would have revealed it when he first theorized about communists being behind the killing on August 21, or when he reported there was a plot. In late September Marcos could tell this story because by then Cawigan had been primed.

And at this point across the scene may have passed the shadow of the ambitious Eduardo Cojuangco, Jr. During the Aquino military trial in 1977, it was this cousin of Corazon Aquino who brought forward several of the witnesses against Aquino.

Cawigan, re-emerging from obscurity, was one of those witnesses.

Unless Marcos had deluded himself, he knew that the military trial of Aquino was rigged with intimidated witnesses and false testimony. Marcos knew then and now that Aquino was neither a communist nor communist sympathizer. He knew that a pivotal point in the government's version of the assassination was that there was a communist plot and Galman was its instrument. Marcos was aware that there was no evidence of such a plot. Thus, the need for Cawigan who Marcos knew was a phoney.

Marcos is not blind. Assuming his participation in the coverup was unwitting, he could not escape the fact that the government's version was rapidly crumbling under the assault of hard fact.

If Marcos were knowingly involved in the coverup from the outset, then he was actively or tacitly a part of the conspiracy to kill Aquino.

If he were unaware of the conspiracy and performed as a spokesman for the coverup because he believed his subordinates, then there had to come a time when his participation was no longer innocent, when any reasonable person would realize there was something very wrong with the Olivas/Ver/Custodio story.

President Marcos could have taken part in the Cawigan concoction – as he obviously did – merely to show that his theory of a communist conspiracy were true. That was conceivable, but not likely. Considerable effort was expended to establish a false story which neatly fitted the gaps in the claim of a plot against Aquino's life. Therefore, in all probability, Cawigan's tale was meant to do more than just prove out a Marcos theory.

The strange thing about the Cawigan caper was that it was so incredibly transparent. Marcos' participation seemed to demonstrate that either he was talked into it by panicky conspirators or he himself was showing signs of losing a grip on the situation. On the other hand, it may have been intended as just another red herring to launch another round of diversionary speculation.

Its importance was Marcos' direct involvement for he put the entire story (without Cawigan's name) on American television. For the first time he did more than theorize or repeat what the military was telling everyone. On the conjugal level it got Imelda Marcos off the hook by giving credence to her claim that her talk with Aquino in May had been a real warning and not a threat.

Whether President Marcos' coverup activity was innocent or not, a more far-reaching question faced him and the future of the Philippines: There was hard evidence of a large "hit squad" in the military hierarchy centered in the various "intelligence" units under the direction of General Fabian Ver either operating independently and out of control or acting with President Marcos' knolwedge and consent.

It seemed highly unlikely that General Ver would dare to set this machinery in motion without the approval of the man who created him. Even with the prime weapon of any totalitarian government – the secret intelligence network – in Ver's possession, Marcos could still break him. Loyalty got the General to the top, and it is doubtful he would risk the wrath of a man so jealous of his authority.

Could Olivas, the two Custodios, Abadilla, Ver, at least several dozen subordinates and an unknown number of high-level and low-level people put together a conspiracy of this magnitude and political impact without Marcos being aware of it? Even after the fact would not the myriad challenges to the government's story cause Marcos to suspect it was all a tissue of lies, particularly when he was involved in one of the fabrications?

Marcos himself provided the answer. In an interview on Manila Channel 4, Associated Press Bureau Chief David Briscoe asked him:

"Mr. President, you said that this (the Aquino murder) could possibly be a communist rubout job. Are you firmly convinced that there's no involvement on the part of anyone in your government in the assassination?"

Marcos: "Yes, on the last part. I am convinced that if any member of my government were involved, I would have known, somehow."

Briscoe: "Even at a fairly low level?"

Marcos: "Even at a fairly low level, I would have known. I know how the soldiers feel. I know how they think. I know what they are thinking of."

It is interesting, if not significant, that Briscoe asked about "anyone in your government" and before he was through, Marcos talked about "the soldiers."

It is possible that this was just braggadocio, an "I know everything that's going on" type of expansive statement. However, in the case of the Aquino assassination conspiracy, he did not have to know what the sergeants and corporals were thinking. He only had to know what the Chief of Staff of the Armed Forces and men of rank between Lieutenant Colonel and Major General were actually doing.

If Ferdinand Marcos, isolated, ill, with a "bunker" mentality, did not know what happened in the most devastating occurrence of his administration, then he may find himself the next target – not just of assassination but of irrelevancy – as the survivors struggle for his faltering sceptre.

Marcos' near perfect performance in furthering the coverup gave credence to his having knowledge of the plot. His willingness to participate in an obvious fabrication indicated his knowledge of the elements of the coverup. The vertical nature of his semi-dictatorial regime made a high-level conspiracy without his knowledge difficult to conceive. That is, unless he was no longer really in charge.

Presuming that Marcos was in control, why would this politically shrewd man take such a gamble to eliminate Aquino? The fears of Aquino as a symbol, campaigner and organizer have been explored. They carried considerable weight with Marcos.

Marcos like Cojuangco, probably actively hated Aquino. Every time Marcos looked for a way to stay in power there was Aquino haunting him. Plaza Miranda was bombed and Aquino was late, Aquino along with Roxas led the liberal slate to substantial gains. Marcos put him in prison, he sentenced him to death, he let Aquino go off to the United States, he took his passport and his Filipino nationality (at least on paper), he warned him, he threatened him, and the man kept coming. Exasperation, frustration and fear – with a good sprinkling of hate – may have overruled the head that said be cautious.

The conspirators believed the chances of pulling off the assassination with little or no proof of their participation were nearly one hundred percent. They would have been right, except for the surprising number of media people, trained to see as much as they could and armed with modern equipment. Marcos, himself, in a moment of insight told reporters that he was bewildered as to why so many reporters accompanied Aquino.

Political assassinations had worked in the past without arrests. As recently as December, 1981, opposition leader Jose Lingad of Pampagna had been shot down in broad daylight by a man in a polo barong who then got back in his pick-up truck and drove away. President Marcos directed the Constabulary to spare no one in going after the killers. The President expressed the theory that the former governor had been slain by the communist New People's Army. No one was ever tried or apprehended.

Similarly, the near fatal shooting of former Vice President Emmanual Pelaez in 1982 (after he criticized the coconut monopoly) resulted in no arrests.

Once there had been an arrest for an alleged political murder – when a young law student named Ferdinand E. Marcos was charged with shooting with an ROTC rifle the man who had just beaten Marcos' father in a provincial election. The date: September 21, 1935. The result: Conviction, overturned by the Philippine Supreme Court and never retried.

Although Marcos knew full well that Aquino was not pro-communist, his charges in 1978 of Aquino being a possible CIA agent were based on his belief that the CIA had extensive influence on American foreign policy. As an Asian he was aware that a secret shift in American policy led to the coup in South Viet Nam in which Premier Diem was executed in the back of a military van.

Marcos' apparent paranoia in this regard could have been exacerbated by two events during the summer. On June 23 Aquino gave a long presentation to the Asian Subcommittee of the House of Representatives predicting disaster for the Philippines without freedom for a legitimate opposition. More devastating to Marcos was the testimony three days later by Assistant Secretary of State Paul Wolfowitz, which mirrored Aquino's sentiments that Marcos should allow the opposition to operate without constraints.

He may have seen the American government's hand, and specifically that of the CIA, in Aquino's insistence on returning. He made no secret of the fact that he wanted Aquino to remain in the United States. To a mind which dealt in conspiracies and depended on the power of secret intelligence, the return of Aquino might look like an American plot to determine the succession.

It may seem strange that numerology could play a part in the decisions of a head of state. While Aquino, in effect, picked his own day of death, the number 21 and the date August 21, in particular, held positive significance for Ferdinand Marcos. Twenty-one was his lucky number. He was charged with murder for a killing on September 21st and was eventually set free. The Plaza Miranda bombing of the Liberal Rally – whoever was responsible – took place on August 21. Martial law was declared on September 21. If the decision to kill Aquino was made after the arrival date of August 21 had been determined – and Marcos knew of the plot – he could have felt the date was an omen of success.

The hard evidence that time and again links the Chief of Staff Ver to the conspiracy, required very little additional deductive reasoning to make Ferdinand Marcos one of the plotters. His systematic participation in the coverup, including orchestrating the Cawigan fiction, added weight to a conclusion of guilt.

If Marcos was not part of the plot then his claims of controlling the government were hollow, his closest advisors had betrayed him, and he had deluded himself in continuing to support their crumbling mosaic of falsehoods.

When Sam Donaldson of ABC on October 2, put the question to him directly, President Marcos fairly spluttered his indignation. This was the exchange:

Donaldson: "Your position has been all along that you had nothing to do with it, and I'm sure you've investigated. Then you are saying that neither you nor anyone in your government nor your wife Imelda Marcos had anything to do with this assassination. Is that correct?"

Marcos: "Let's not be ridiculous. Why should we want to kill Aquino? That's the most joking suggestion ever made."

It was on this same program that Marcos first planted the Cawigan story.

If President Marcos continues to protest his own innocence and deny a governmental conspiracy exists despite the evidence, he owes a final debt to his native land: To cleanse his name of the Macbethian blot caused by Senator Aquino's murder.

When the authors began this analysis, they believed with Jose Diokno, that President Marcos "would never have had Ninoy killed the way he was." The overwhelming weight of consistent, interlocking evidence has placed President Marcos squarely in the middle of the conspiracy. Whether he chooses to take action to promote a complete, effective investigation is up to him.

If President Marcos chooses not to, the indelible record of blood described here will speak for itself.

Ninoy Aquino In His Own Words

Is Ninoy Aquino a hero and a martyr who sacrificed his life for the peace and freedom of his countrymen or was he a politician who gambled his life to satisfy his own selfish ambitions and lost?

One can form one's own impressions and conclusions by learning more about the person's life and what he had to say. Ninoy Aquino was a prolific writer. To those who knew him well, Ninoy's beliefs and convictions are best represented by the following mosaic of quotations from many writings during the past 12 years.

The Filipino is worth dying for

* * *

These I hold sacred: the inherent dignity and worth of every human being, his freedom of thought and speech and press, his liberty to choose – without fear or pressure – the public officials of his own choice, and the great principles of democracy handed down to us by our forebears....

* * *

... My heart and mind and my soul – yes, every part of my being is against any form of dictatorship. I agree we must have public order and national discipline, if the country is to move forward. But peace and order without freedom is nothing more than slavery. Discipline without justice is merely another name for oppression. I believe we can have lasting peace and prosperity only if we build a social order based on freedom and justice. My non-participation in the proceedings of my trial is . . . an act of protest against the structures of injustice that brought us here. It is also an act of faith in the ultimate victory of right over wrong, of good over evil. In all humility, I say it is a rare privilege to share with the Motherland her bondage, her anguish, her every pain and suffering.

The struggle in the Philippines today is between those who have been mesmerized by the 'efficiency' of authoritarianism and those who still hold that democracy with all its flaws and inefficiency is man's best hope for betterment and progress. Man's sense of justice makes democracy possible; man's injustice makes it necessary.

We must teach our people to respond, not merely to react. We must tell them, to the point of being repetitious – we must criticize to be free, because we are free only when we criticize.

We must tell them to be not mere objects of history. They must be history's creator. We must remind them of the constant need for their martyrs, if we are to create ever better tomorrows.

* * *

I believe the cause delaying our liberation may be found in ourselves; in our reluctance to assert our rights and frontally confront the forces of evil. We are afraid to die and our fear has immobilized us. We have forged our own chains with our cowardice! . . .

I have decided to challenge death. I do not believe I'm sinning against my Creator because in the end, I am not really my own executioner.

* * *

Our people need courage more than ever. They will have to risk the possibility of being picked up in the night, of losing their jobs and even the security of their homes. But I assure them that their sublime courage, their willingness to suffer and their dedication and determination in the midst of great provocations will qualify them as the real heroes of our time.

Those who have the force of arms will win in the meanwhile. But they will surely lose in the end. For to paraphrase Unamuno, the great thinker, for them to finally prevail, they must convince; to convince, they have to persuade; and in order to persuade, *they need what they do not and cannot have: right and reason in the crucial struggle.*

*   *   *

The Filipino today is facing an ever-deepening crisis. Never in history has he suffered from greater political and economic wants. It is time for every Filipino abroad who loves his country to return home, suffer with his people and help in the quest for that elusive national unity which is imperative for the nation's survival.

*   *   *

...Communism may be defeated not by adopting the brutal methods of the enemy and thereby lose your moral imperative, but by reinforcing human rights. One can fight hatred with greater hatred, but Magsaysay proved that it is more effective to fight hatred with greatest Christian love.

*   *   *

I have chosen to return to the silence of my solitary confinement and from there work for a peaceful solution to our problems rather than come back triumphant to the blare of trumpets and cymbals seeking to drown the wailings and sad lamentations of mothers whose sons and daughters have been sacrificed to the gods of revolution. Can the killers of today be the leaders of tomorrow? Must we destroy in order to build? I refuse to believe that it is necessary for a nation to build its foundation on the bones of its young.

*   *   *

What is more tragic, in the midst of all these miseries, Filipinos are killing each other in ever-increasing numbers. This blood-letting must stop. This madness must cease.

I think it can be stopped if all Filipinos can get together as true brothers and sisters and search for a healing solution, in a genuine spirit of give and take. We must transcend our petty selves, forget our hurts and bitterness, cast aside thoughts of revenge and let sanity, reason, and above all, love of country prevail during our gravest hour.

211

Subversion stems from economic, social and political causes and will not be solved by purely military solutions; it can be curbed not with ever-increasing repression but with a more equitable distribution of wealth, more democracy and more freedom. And for the economy to get going once again, the workingman must be given his just and rightful share of his labor, and to the owners and managers must be restored hope where there is so much uncertainty if not despair.

I remain resolute...I know I am guilty of nothing, except to have stood up to the would-be dictator. If such will be the price I'll have to pay, so be it. A time comes in a man's life when he must prefer a meaningful death to a meaningless life. I would rather die on my feet with honor, than live on bended knees in shame.

* * *

NINOY AQUINO'S FINAL MESSAGE

Why did Aquino return to the Philippines expecting to face, at best, solitary confinement in prison and, at worse, death? Again, one can speculate on his reasons but one can at least read Aquino's own answer. His answer is contained in a prepared statement he was planning to deliver to his welcomers upon his arrival at the Manila International Airport, as printed in the *New York Times*, August 22, 1983.

I have returned on my free will to join the ranks of those struggling to restore our rights and freedoms through nonviolence.

I seek no confrontation. I only pray and will strive for a genuine national reconciliation founded on justice.

I am prepared for the worst, and have decided against the advice of my mother, my spiritual adviser, many of my tested friends and a few of my most valued political mentors.

A death sentence awaits me. Two more subversion charges, both calling for death penalties, have been filed since I left three years ago and are now pending with the courts.

I could have opted to seek political asylum in America, but I feel it is my duty, as it is the duty of every Filipino, to suffer with his people especially in time of crisis.

I never sought nor have I been given any assurances or promise of leniency by the regime. I return voluntarily armed only with a clear conscience and fortified in the faith that in the end justice will emerge triumphant.

According to Gandhi, the willing sacrifice of the innocent is the most powerful answer to insolent tyranny that has yet been conceived by God and man.

Three years ago, when I left for an emergency heart by-pass operation, I hoped and prayed that the rights and freedoms of our people would soon be restored, that living conditions would improve and that bloodletting would stop.

Rather than move forward, we have moved backward. The killings have increased, the economy has taken a turn for the worse and the human-rights situation has deteriorated.

During the martial-law period, the Supreme Court heard petitions for habeas corpus. It is most ironic after martial law has allegedly been lifted, that the Supreme Court last April ruled it can no longer entertain petitions for habeas corpus for persons detained under a Presidential Commitment Order, which covers all so-called national security cases and which under present circumstances can cover almost anything.

The country is far advanced in her times of trouble. Economic, social and political problems bedevil the Filipino. These problems may be surmounted if we are united. But we can be united only if all the rights and freedoms enjoyed before Sept. 21, 1972 are fully restored.

The Filipino asked for nothing more, but will surely accept nothing less, than all the rights and freedoms guaranteed by the 1935 constitution – the most sacred legacies from the founding fathers.

Yes, the Filipino is patient, but there is a limit to his patience. Must we wait until that patience snaps?

The nationwide rebellion is escalating and threatens to explode into a bloody revolution. There is a growing cadre of young Filipinos who have finally come to realize that freedom is never granted, it is taken. Must we relive the agonies and the bloodletting of the past that brought forth our republic or can we sit down as brothers and sisters and discuss our differences with reason and goodwill?

I have often wondered how many disputes could have been settled easily had the disputants only dared to define their terms.

So as to leave no room for misunderstanding, I shall define my terms:

1. Six years ago, I was sentenced to die before a firing squad by a military tribunal whose jurisdiction I steadfastly refused to recognize. It is now time for the regime to decide. Order my immediate execution or set me free.

I was sentenced to die for allegedly being the leading Communist leader. I am not a Communist, never was and never will be.

2. National reconciliation and unity can be achieved but only with justice, including justice for our Moslem and Ifugao brothers. There can be no deal with a dictator. No compromise with dictatorship.

3. In a revolution there can really be no victors, only victims. We do not have to destroy in order to build.

4. Subversion stems from economic, social and political causes and will not be solved by purely military solutions; it can be curbed not with ever increasing repression but with a more equitable distribution of wealth, more democracy and more freedom.

5. For the economy to get going once again, the working man must be given his just and rightful share of his labor, and to the owners and managers must be restored the hope where there is so much uncertainty if not despair.

On one of the long corridors of Harvard University are carved in granite the words of Archibald MacLeish: "How shall freedom by defended? By arms when it is attacked by arms; by truth when it is attacked by lies, by democratic faith when it is attacked by authoritarian dogma. Always, and in the final act, by determination and faith."

214

I return from exile and to an uncertain future with only determination and faith to offer – faith in our people and faith in God.

Commentary

by Steve Psinakis, Director
Ninoy Aquino Movement for Freedom, Peace and Democracy
(NAMFPD)

The close examination of the Aquino assassination by the investigative team of the Ninoy Aquino movement has established the complicity of Philippine Government agents in general and high-ranking officials in particular. Through their own independent analysis of the evidence, the authors of *The Aquino Assassination* reached the same basic conclusion. The responsibility for the crime falls directly and totally on Mr. Marcos even under the (very) remote possibility that the decision to assassinate Senator Aquino originated with someone other than Mr. Marcos.

As the truth about the complicity of the Marcos regime becomes better known and accepted throughout the Philippines, the United States and the rest of the world, the current Philippine crisis will evolve into its "next phase". Political observers of the Philippine scene are raising questions and speculating on the probable alternative scenarios of the "next phase".

In the light of the Philippine Government's complicity to the assassination, Mr. Marcos' options are rather limited. Essentially, Mr. Marcos will (a) yield to the popular demand of the people to relinquish the reigns of government or (b) attempt to ride the crisis and hold on to his authoritarian rule.

(a) Graceful way out;
return democratic rule through honest elections.

Mr. Marcos has an excellent opportunity to relinquish power gracefully and peacefully through the process of general national elections. He can grant the Philippine people the right to elect their

216

government officials, including their President, through genuinely honest and free elections.

A simplified but concrete scenario under which this option may be implemented would be for Mr. Marcos to announce that, in the spirit of national reconciliation and/or for reasons of health, he and his wife will retire from politics. Following the announcement of his retirement, Mr. Marcos would institute the prerequisites for sincere reconciliation and honest elections, i.e., release all political prisoners; restore press freedom; revamp the Commission on Elections (COM-ELEC); accredit the political parties; revise the election rules, etc.

While the above scenario is, admittedly, over-simplified, its main components are clearly defined and must be contained in any of a number of other possible scenarios acceptable to Mr. Marcos, to the opposition leaders and, most importantly, to the people of the Philippines.

The basic and essential component of this option is the decision of Mr. Marcos to step down gracefully and allow the establishment of a free democratic government through peaceful means – free and honest elections.

In honor of the sacrifice and ideals of Senator Aquino, several leaders of the moderate opposition, including members of the Aquino family, are known to favor a peaceful transition to democracy, rather than revenge for the assassination. Should Mr. Marcos decide to withdraw gracefully and allow free elections, the crisis brought about by the assassination may be defused and may be resolved by the arrest and prosecution of the military officer(s) and men who actually committed the murder.

(b) Remain in power;
ride the crisis through total crackdown.

Mr. Marcos can decide to remain in power, thus reinforcing the people's perception that he is determined to perpetuate his family dynasty at any cost.

In such an event, the Marcos regime will have to suppress the people's massive movement through a new crackdown which may become much more brutal than the repressive measures employed during the years of martial rule, i.e. resort to sweeping arrests of opposition leaders and "subversives" who are demanding his resignation; ban all demonstrations and punish the "agitators"; re-impose curfews, etc.

A decision to remain in power will, by necessity, also mean the complete whitewash of the investigation of the Aquino assassination. Mr. Marcos will have to declare his government free of any complicity and insist on the fabrication of the communist plot theory, executed by the "lone assassin" Rolando Galman.

Considering the vast evidence which proves the impossibility of the "lone assassin" scenario, some observers believe that Mr. Marcos could decide to use a low-ranking military officer as the "scapegoat" of a conspiracy which did not involve high-ranking officials of his government.

However, most observers believe that while a "scapegoat" approach may have been credible at an early stage of the investigation, Mr. Marcos and his top generals are now too deeply embroiled in the on-going cover-up. Consequently, any attempt to exonerate themselves at this late stage through a low level "scapegoat" would lack as much credibility as the "lone assassin" fabrication.

The option to remain in power through force will have to do away with any pretense of accountability to the people or concern for human rights and democratic processes. This option will rely solely on the power and brute force of the military establishment.

The Filipino People Have Spoken.

During the past several years, the Marcos Government has been gradually approaching a serious political and economic crisis. The assassination of Senator Aquino brought the crisis to a breaking point. The solution to the crisis rests in the hands of the Filipino people.

The general public's belief that the Marcos regime is responsible for the assassination of Senator Aquino has generated massive but peaceful demonstrations. The people have chosen to pursue the ideals and goals of their fallen leader by resorting only to peaceful demands for the dismantling of the dictatorship and the return of a truly democratic government. The demonstrations and other means of civil disobedience are expected to continue until Mr. Marcos either yields to the people's demands or resorts to the brutal crackdown.

The Role of the U.S. Government

Whether the Filipino and American people like it or not, the U.S. Government has no choice but to play a significant role in the resolution of the present Philippine crisis. The U.S. Government's options are also very limited; basically only two: (a) a policy of interfering in the domestic affairs of the Philippines and (b) a policy of non-interference.

(a) *U.S. Interference.*

Concerned about the unknowns of a free and independent democratic government in the Philippines, the U.S. Government may decide to interfere by encouraging Mr. Marcos to crackdown and maintain the "status quo" with the assurance of full U.S. economic and military support for his regime.

In such an event, it is very probable that the present momentum of the people for the restoration of democracy through peaceful means will suffer an irreversible and permanent setback. The Marcos regime will be temporarily rescued and will remain in power for an additional one, two, three or a maximum of five to six years. The moderate forces will lose all hope for a peaceful change and will join the radical elements who are already engaged in the revolutionary road to liberation. The ultimate result will be a victory of the revolutionary forces after the customary destruction and loss of life which characterize all protracted revolutions. The emerging government will necessarily be radically anti-American (and most probably of the extreme left) resulting in the U.S. loss of a traditional ally and the loss of all U.S. interests in the Philippines.

(b) *U.S. non-interference.*

The U.S. Government may decide to adopt a policy of non-interference by informing Mr. Marcos *now* – through quiet diplomatic channels – that it cannot and will not interfere to rescue the Marcos regime by supplying it with economic and military assistance which will be used for internal conflicts. In effect, the U.S. Government will inform Mr. Marcos that the free will of the Filipino people must be respected and that America will not provide Mr. Marcos with the economic and military wherewithal to enable him to suppress the will of his own people. If the U.S. Government made its position clear to Mr. Marcos, it is very unlikely that he would risk the "crackdown" option which, without U.S. support, is bound to fail.

It appears that the Reagan Administration has made its decision on this issue. The State Department announced its policy with regard to the present Philippine crisis during the September 13, 1983, Congressional Hearings on the Aquino assassination before the Subcommittee on Asian and Pacific Affairs of the House Foreign Affairs Committee.

Having acquiesced on the issue of assuring Senator Aquino's "safety" upon his return – a fact which some observers, including this writer, believe contributed to the Aquino assassination – the Reagan Administration appears to have decided that it will not commit the same error again.

During the September Congressional Hearings, the U.S. Department of State, through its Deputy Assistant Secretary John Monjo, made the following statement before the House Foreign Affairs Subcommittee in regard to the assassination:

> The Aquino assassination has rocked the Philippines. It was a tragic event that has beclouded the reputation of the Philippine government. *Many Filipinos, and not all of them opposed to the current government, suspect the complicity of elements in the government in the crime* [Emphasis added]. It raises very disturbing questions that demand answers. It puts into grave doubt the competence of the airport security forces, who themselves are suspect of at best gross negligence in their duties. We do not have the answers to those questions yet. As we have stated, we look to the Government of the Philippines to provide them.
>
> This is a matter, first and foremost, that concerns the Philippine government and the Philippine people. But the United States Government has made clear to the Government of the Philippines both publicly and privately that, in view of our close relationship, the United States also has and continues to have the deepest concern over the assassination of Senator Aquino. *We fully expect the Philippine Government to act swiftly and vigorously to track down the perpetrators of this crime, as President Marcos promised in his statement on the day of the murder.* [Emphasis added]
>
> At this point, we still know very little about the assassination that is not already a matter of public record. Not enough evidence has yet been found to substantiate or to rule out any of the several possible explanations which have been mentioned so far. *The circumstances of the murder and the identity of the alleged assassin, whom the GOP* [Government of the Philippines] *describes as "a notorious killer, a gun for hire," make us doubt that one man alone could have been responsible for this clearly political assassination.* [Emphasis added]

Regarding the elections, Undersecretary Monjo stated the Administration's position as follows:

> With the assassination of Senator Aquino, the opposition has lost its most charismatic leader. *Senator Aquino had hoped to return home to persuade the Marcos Government and his fellow members of the opposition to find electoral solutions to the Philippine's political problems* [Emphasis added]. Now that Senator Aquino is gone, the leaders of the moderate opposition must decide what they will do. The Marcos Government, for it part, will also have to decide on how to deal with the new political situation as it prepares for the 1984 parliamentary election.
>
> We cannot foretell how the political events will play out. For our part, we hope that both the government and the moderate opposition will deal with this new political reality in a way that contributes to political stability, the strengthening of democratic institutions, and respect for human rights. In this regard *it is more important than ever that the May, 1984, parliamentary election be one in which the legitimate opposition will have a free and fair opportunity to participate* [Emphasis added]. If the ground rules for the election permit the legitimate opposition to participate, then it could be the most significant electoral exercise in the Philippines since the declaration of martial law in 1972.

In addition to the declaration of the State Department's position, the U.S. House of Representatives also approved a Resolution by an unprecedented bypartisan vote of 413 to 3 calling for: (1) "a thorough, independent, and impartial; investigation of the Aquino assassination in a timely fashion" and (2) "genuine, free and fair elections to the National Assembly in May 1984". . . . with "the full participation of the opposition parties in these elections, including the prompt reconstitution of an objective, impartial electoral commission and restoration of full freedom of the press".

The House Resolution also stated that "the United States Government should take into account, among other factors, the conduct of the Government of the Philippines' investigation into the Aquino assassination and the fairness of the 1984 National Assembly elections in the conduct of its relations with the Government of the Philippines".

The House Resolution will be taken up by the U.S. Senate soon after its Christmas holiday recess. Consequently, the Reagan Administration will be further pressed by the Congress to maintain a clearly defined position on the investigation of the assassination and on the conduct of the elections.

"Time Running Out"

Just prior to his assassination, Senator Aquino stated that "time is running out" for a peaceful resolution to the Philippine crisis.

While there is significant difference of opinion on whether the Philippine problem will finally be resolved through peaceful or violent means, there is hardly any difference or opinion on whether "time is running out".

What are the prospects of peace versus violence? The Filipino people have lit the fuse which will lead to the dismantling of the Marcos regime either through the road of peace or through a violent explosion. Mr. Marcos and the U.S. Government have to decide where their best interests lie and which of their respective options will lead them in that direction.

About the Authors

Gerald N. Hill has been a practicing California attorney for more than 25 years and has been active in politics for three decades. He is the co-author and editor of *Housing in California* and wrote *The Democratic Crisis* about American policy in southeast Asia. Mr. Hill served as a special advisor for A.I.D. in Latin America. He is a graduate of Stanford University and the University of California's Hastings College of the Law.

Kathleen Thompson Hill is the author and editor of many articles and books on a variety of subjects. A graduate of the University of California at Berkeley with a Certificat from the Sorbonne, Mrs. Hill was a Coro Foundation Fellow in Public Affairs and worked for the Peace Corps in Washington and at the White House in 1963. She was Coordinator of the 25th Anniversary of the United Nations in San Francisco and served on a California Grand Jury for the year 1982–83.

Both of the Hills have a long history of concern for human rights and democracy in the Philippines. Having travelled widely in the Philippines, Mrs. Hill is one of a relatively few Americans who has met Senator Aquino as well as President and Mrs. Marcos.

Steve Psinakis, Director of the Ninoy Aquino Movement for Freedom, Peace and Democracy, lived in the Philippines for a decade while employed in the top management of the industrial empire of the late Eugenio Lopez, Sr. During that period he became acquainted with many local and foreign business executives as well as political leaders including Mr. and Mrs. Ferdinand Marcos.

A naturalized American citizen of Greek origin, Mr. Psinakis is married to Presentacion (Presy) Lopez Psinakis. Shortly after the political imprisonment of his brother-in-law, Eugenio (Geny) Lopez, Jr. in Fort Bonifacio, Psinakis became active in the effort to restore human rights and democracy to the Philippines.

In 1977, he was instrumental in the escape of Geny Lopez and Sergio Osmena, III from Fort Bonifacio and their sensational flight to freedom in the United States. He is the author of a book, *Two Terrorists Meet*, which relates his negotiations and confrontations with Imelda Marcos in the United States.

An engineer by training, Psinakis is a graduate of the University of Pittsburgh. He and his family reside in San Francisco.

Gerald N. Hill

Kathleen Thompson Hill

Steve Psinakis